D1716442

ACOUSTICS OF WORSHIP SPACES

ACOUSTICS OF WORSHIP SPACES

Presented at the 106th Meeting of the
ACOUSTICAL SOCIETY OF AMERICA
San Diego, 7–11 November 1983

Edited by

David Lubman
D. Lubman & Associates
Westminster, California

Ewart A. Wetherill
Bolt Beranek and Newman, Inc.
Canoga Park, California

Published by the American Institute of Physics
for the Acoustical Society of America

Library of Congress Catalog Card Number: 85-70293
International Standard Book Number: 0-88318-466-4

Published by the American Institute of Physics, Inc.
335 East 45 Street, New York, New York 10017

Printed in the United States of America

TABLE OF CONTENTS

INTRODUCTION

1. For Whom this Book is Intended

This book is intended primarily for people involved in the practical acoustical planning of worship space interiors of buildings such as chapels, churches, mosques, temples, and synagogues. Acousticians, architects, building committees, clergy, choir and music directors, and sound system designers are among the intended audience.

2. The Uses of this Book

From these drawings, photographs, and accompanying data one may gain insight into the nature of worship space acoustics and its current practice. In this book readers will find a rich variety in the approach taken to worship space acoustics arising from differences of denominational and congregational style and budget. Within each style, the alert reader will also find recurring issues, problems, approaches, and compromises arising from an underlying similarity of concerns, objectives, and technology.

Readers involved in planning their own projects may find more immediate and practical benefit from this collection and distillation of worship space project experiences. We hope they may harvest valuable ideas and inspirations for the prevention as well as the solution of a wide variety of worship space acoustical problems.

Since the projects shown cover a wide variety of new construction and renovations made over a narrow span of time and also cover a broad denominational base, this collection can also be seen as a period piece documenting current acoustical practice in sacred architecture circa 1983.

To increase the value of this book for those persons with little background in acoustics, we have included brief essays on some aspects of worship space acoustics that are implied by the recurring themes inherent in the Poster Papers.

3. How it Came About

The collection of drawings, photographs, and technical data on worship facilities contained herein is an outgrowth of three Special Sessions organized around the theme "Acoustics of Worship Spaces," which took place at the 106th Meeting of the Acoustical Society of America, 7–11 November 1983 at the Town and Country Hotel in San Diego, California. The theme was organized by the Technical Committee on Architectural Acoustics, with the participation of the Technical Committee on Musical Acoustics and other elements of the Acoustical Society.

The theme's centerpiece was a Poster Session that presented in visual form over forty acoustical projects involving worship facilities as described by the acoustical consultants and architects who were responsible for them. The Posters—on display throughout the meeting—drew enthusiastic audiences from all disciplines of acoustics, as well as architects, musicians, and related professionals from throughout the United States and abroad.

Related sessions on "Organ Technology Today" and "Architectural Acoustics for the Organ" rounded out the theme.

4. What the Poster Papers Tell Us

The Poster Papers collected for this publication show sectional and plan drawings of worship space interiors, using standardized scales throughout. Architectural drawings are supplemented with photographs intended to aid in their interpretation and to provide an overall impression of the finished interior. A visual format was chosen to facilitate communication with architects and others involved in the practical planning of worship space interiors. The standardized scales were chosen to facilitate rapid visual comparison of different facilities. A one-page written description of each project is also included. This *fact sheet* identifies the building, architect, acoustical consultant, and project completion date. In some cases a brief description of acoustical design features and measured data is included. In a few cases, a concise statement of the problem, objective, and approach is also provided.

ACKNOWLEDGMENTS

The contributors of Poster Papers that appear herein are the primary "heroes" of this book, and their material is its primary substance. Each Poster Paper is a labor of pride and of love whose production only the most passionately dedicated professionals would complete. They have our admiration and respect.

Enthusiastic members and friends of the ASA's Technical Committee on Architectural Acoustics deserve our gratitude, for it was they who conceived, sponsored, planned, and executed the Poster Session. William J. Cavanaugh originated the idea that led to our first published Poster Presentation, "Halls for Music Performance: 1962–1982." He and co-editors Richard H. Talaske and Ewart A. Wetherill provided the advice and encouragement out of which this volume was born.

Ronald L. McKay served as Poster Session Co-Chairman, participating in its planning and execution until business plans forced his resignation in favor of Ewart "Red" Wetherill—who had been quietly rendering competent assistance to planners and Poster authors all along. Red gets all the credit for overseeing the transformation of Posters into photographs, the design of the book cover, and my eternal gratitude for his numerous labors on behalf of this book, each done with flair, enthusiasm, good taste, and cheer.

At the San Diego ASA Meeting where the Posters were on display all week, Jim Dukes of Sound Transmision Control, Inc. was responsible for Poster arrangements. He provided easels, Poster check-in, mailing, and storage services, and a generous wine and cheese reception for Poster authors. San Diego AIA Chapter President Ralph Bradshaw provided liaison with local architects for this reception. Ralph, along with Robert S. Gales and Robert W. Young, provided the information used for planning the bus tour of local churches. Others helped too. For example, at the end of the week, during a brief lapse in the arrangements, David Pallett helped to rescue the unguarded Posters from possible damage.

A special note of appreciation goes to Birgit Nystrom for her infinite patience in preparing the project fact sheets, and to the Canoga Park office of Bolt Beranek and Newman, Inc., for providing her services.

The Acoustical Society of America sponsored this special project. Publication experts Kenneth Dreyhaupt and Larry Feinberg of the American Institute of Physics advised on and assisted with its production.

David Lubman

Considerations for the Design of Worship Space Acoustics: An Acoustical Consultant's Viewpoint

David L. Klepper
Klepper Marshall King Associates, Ltd.
White Plains, NY 10603

As in any building where speech and music are both important considerations, the proper acoustical design of a particular worship space depends on the *type* of music performed, the importance of *speech* intelligibility in the particular services, and on the *size* and other architectural characteristics of the space. There is no one simple solution to providing good acoustics for both speech and music, not even for a worship space of a particular size.

The range of variation in the acoustical design of worship spaces may be illustrated by describing four very different architectural and liturgical styles.

Cathedral Style

The *cathedral* style is a large worship space housing an impressive pipe organ. Here, choir music, congregational singing, and responses are all important. Of course, speech must be intelligible, but at the same time a long reverberation period is required for the music portion of the service. Hard sound-reflecting surfaces are required for the congregation to hear themselves sing, and a basically hard, sound-reflecting space is required to complement the cathedral-style architecture. Good speech intelligibility requires a carefully designed sound system regardless of whether the space is acoustically "live" or "dead," so this consultant opts for the "live" solution, with perhaps a three- or four-second reverberation time when occupied, and an electronic speech amplification system that concentrates the amplified speech energy over the (sound-absorbing) congregation seating area, and avoids directing amplified sound toward hard wall and ceiling surfaces. Such a system may employ large directional loudspeakers in a central cluster, loudspeakers directed downward and distributed in chandeliers, distributed and digitally delayed loudspeakers on columns or even digitally delayed pew-back speakers with one small loudspeaker for every three or four worshipers.

Intimate Meeting House Style

At the opposite acoustical extreme we may have a small, low *meeting house* style of worship space with an electronic or pipe organ. Music may be important here too, but the "intimate" style of architecture rules out a long reverberation time. The short distances mean that speech can be intelligible without electronic amplification, at least for people who speak well. The house's musical program should feature music that thrills in an intimate acoustical environment, with a reverberation time in the 0.8–1.2-second range when occupied. Sound-absorbing material should be used sparingly, if at all, and the architect should be encouraged to use hard surfaces creatively to control echo and maximize speech intelligibility and uniformity of sound distribution.

Evangelical Style

A third architectural and liturgical style, very different from either of the above, is the *large evangelical church*. It may have as large a volume as the cathedral, but its acoustical design must reflect a distinctly different style of music and preaching. Here, an electronic organ and a piano are the major musical instruments; the style of music resembles contemporary popular music more than traditional liturgical music, and preachers employ a wide dynamic range of voice level. All music and speech is amplified. Since often the service is televised, the entire church can be viewed as a large television sound studio. The acoustical architecture of a large evangelical church should resemble a conventional-style auditorium more than a traditional cathedral. By judicious application of sound-absorbing materials, the architectural acoustic design should seek to achieve a reverberation time in the 1.0–1.5-second range at mid-frequencies when occupied. The sound systems of large Evangelical churches often resemble those of popular music theatres.

Concert Hall Style

The three architectural/liturgical styles described above are meant to represent extremes. Obviously, there are intermediate cases between them. In particular, a moderately-sized house with a strong musical program and a requirement for high speech intelligibility might best be served by a *concert-hall acoustics environment*, which we take as our fourth style of worship space. This style will usually require a reverberation time of around 1.8–2.0 seconds when occupied, a fairly straightforward electronic speech reinforcement system usually employing a central loudspeaker cluster, and natural acoustics for music.

We have identified above four different styles of worship space, each having its own reverberation time requirements and its own complementary sound system requirements. The acoustical factors that are common to nearly all of these types of worship spaces are now reviewed, with exceptions noted, as required.

Organ and Choir Locations

A good rule is to group the organ, organ console, piano (if any), and all singers and instruments within a 20-foot radius to avoid acoustical time-delay problems. A relatively small choir should be located within forty feet of the organ pipes, if possible. Many houses employ one musician, who may often conduct the choir from the organ bench, to serve as both organist and choir director. For the sake of his musical artistry and acoustical comfort, the director must hear the organ without excessive time delay and must also be close enough to hear the choir with as little time delay as possible. Even if the organist and choir director are two individuals, keeping them in close proximity will assist the coordination of choir and organ.

The pianist (if any) should be close by as part of the same team. An exception to the rule of grouping all singers and instruments, including organ pipes, within a 20-foot radius arises in the cases of antiphonal organs and antiphonal choirs. These are intended for special effects or for keeping the congregation singing together along the length of the church. Antiphonal choirs and organs pose specific problems for the musicians involved and should be avoided when the antiphonal effect is not required.

Best locations for the organ and choir are behind the altar, on the front wall or upstage chancel wall, facing the congregation, or in a reasonably high rear balcony or gallery. In either case, the organ and choir should face down the main axis of the church, with good line of sight to the director and most of the congregation. The choir should be in one group, if possible, immediately below the organ pipes or electronic organ loudspeakers. Less satisfactory are divided chancels, with the choir members at right angles to the congregation and facing each other. Also less satisfactory is placement of the choir or the organ in transepts.

Nearly all organ builders prefer their instruments to be free standing, exposed, and not in so-called organ chambers. Organs today may have free-standing pipes or pipes located in casework (the casework usually consists of wood paneling). Casework should not be thought of as another organ chamber, because the casework will transmit low-frequency sound. Usually, some space should be left at the sides and behind the organ to allow for servicing.

Both the choir and organ (and any piano) should be somewhat elevated with respect to the congregation. In a small worship space, this may be accomplished by a platform and/or choir risers. In some worship spaces, the balcony location provides this elevation.

Avoid placing choir members under very low ceilings. Ceiling heights in the 20–30-foot range are best to provide a mixing of choir voices and their reflections, and to direct choir sound to the congregation. In cathedral-like spaces with higher ceilings, nearby side walls can provide the close-in reflections necessary for good choir communication. Some acoustical shaping of the side walls and ceiling over the choir is often desirable, but cannot always be integrated into an architect's visual design.

Avoidance of Echo and Focusing

Concave rear walls should be avoided, of course, just as in theatres and concert halls. Rear walls that might produce echo should be "broken-up" with a series of splays, undulations, zig-zagging, etc., of a sufficient scale to scatter sound. The use of sound-absorbing material to control echo should be avoided, if possible, in all but evangelical-type churches, where the rear-wall echo control treatment may be part of an overall treatment to provide a low reverberation time. In houses that employ traditional liturgical music, break-up (diffusion) is the proper means to control rear-wall echo.

Vaulted ceilings in cathedral-style spaces are usually high enough so that sound focusing will occur well above the ears of congregation, clergy, and musicians, and such a ceiling may be left hard and sound reflecting. Lower barrel-vault ceilings in colonial-style worship spaces often cause severe focusing effects with "hot spots" and "dead spots." The best solutions to this focusing problem are (1) the addition of coffering or other forms of sound diffusion to the ceiling and (2) changing the curvature of the barrel-vault for small-radius, sharp curves at the sides, and a broad-radius curve, with a radius several times the height of the ceiling, in the center portion. This consultant has used both techniques with success.

Applicable Materials

Most interior finishes of worship spaces are intentionally chosen to be hard and sound reflecting. These hard interior surfaces should reflect sound energy at all frequencies. Because thin wood paneling is a poor reflector of sound at low frequencies its use should be avoided, unless bonded to masonry or gypsum board. Brick, stone and concrete are all good interior materials for worship spaces. If wood panels are used for ceilings, care should be taken to insure that cracks do not develop as the building ages. Plaster is a good material, but it should be relatively thick and heavy. The use of single layers of 1/2- or 5/8-inch gypsum board should be avoided; use two or more layers if possible.

The architectural surfaces near the musical elements (choir, organ, piano) should all be hard and sound reflecting. This means elimination or minimization of carpet in these areas. Exceptions to this rule may be houses that use extensive amplification of music, where sound-absorbing materials may be applicable to give the sound system and broadcasting operators better control.

When sound-absorbing materials must be used, they should be effective throughout a broad frequency range. So-called acoustic plaster has no place in a worship space, since it absorbs only high-frequency energy without absorbing mid-frequency and low-frequency energy. To achieve broad frequency range sound absorption, the use of glass fiber over an air space behind a sound-transparent facing is the most frequently applicable treatment. Since, almost without exception, the *ceiling* is the *last* place to apply sound-absorbing treatment in a worship space, acoustic tile has very little use here.

Pew Cushions and Carpet

Pew cushions definitely reduce the effectiveness of congregational singing, as compared with hard pews. Yet, pew cushions are often essential to control the increase in reverberation time that results with reduced occupancy. The decision whether or not to use pew cushions should be made on a case-by-case basis. At times, even in a large reverberant space, the use of a zoned sound system with "zoned seating" can eliminate the need for pew cushions. (With "zoned seating," the congregation in a partially occupied house are seated together in one zone, and all speech loudspeakers that cover unoccupied areas are switched off.) Upholstered pews are normal for evangelical churches with amplified music.

In spaces where high reverberation times are desired, carpet should be avoided. Carpet absorbs high-frequency energy and reduces the effectiveness of congregational singing and responses. Even small, intimate worship spaces should usually avoid carpeting. Evangelical churches with amplified music may be an exception. However, even in such churches, carpet may be a poor idea for the choir area.

Good Acoustics for What Purpose?

The first step in providing good acoustics for a worship space is to answer the question: "Good acoustics for what purpose?" For a million-dollar pipe organ? For a boys choir? For a preacher with a tremendous dynamic range? For an amplified Gospel choir? For television broadcasts? For all of the above? (A tough requirement.) From the answers to these questions one can then determine optimum reverberation time, the overall acoustical design, and the design of the sound system. Let us also not neglect the importance of good noise control and sound isolation. But even there, no single criterion is applicable to every situation.

Notes on Conflicting Acoustical Requirements for Speech and Music in Worship Spaces, and the Uses of Electronics for their Reconciliation

David Lubman
D. Lubman & Associates
14301 Middletown Lane
Westminster, CA 92683

The conflict between the acoustical requirements favoring music and speech will be seen as one of the major recurring themes in these Poster Papers. A compromise between these competing requirements must be found before beginning the design or renovation of a worship space. Since the compromise should strongly reflect an individual congregation's style, taste, and budget, it is essential for all concerned to understand what is at stake in making this choice. For this purpose, it is important to understand that the explanation for this conflict resides as much in church history as it does in acoustical science.

Historical Note on the Conflict Between Speech and Music in Worship Spaces

Much traditional liturgical music for organ and choir written from the period of the Middle Ages through the Renaissance sounds best in the highly reverberant cathedral spaces for which they were composed. It appears that great cathedral music such as the Gregorian Chant of the Middle Ages and the antiphonal brass music of the Renaissance were marvelous adaptations to the reverberant environments of their day. For listeners, experiencing the reverberant environment of a cathedral can be impressive and moving; one may be hushed into reverential silence. It is a physical property of highly reverberant space that all voices whether near or distant tend to sound equally loud. This may be seen as an acoustical expression of the religious concept that all souls are equal in God's house. For all their majesty, however, highly reverberant cathedral spaces are hostile to intelligible speech (and some hold that their reverberation is excessive even for period music). Since the spoken word in medieval cathedral service consisted only of Latin texts recited by clerics who already knew them well, there was little need for the faithful in the congregation to understand speech.

The practice of singing psalms and responsorial chants at religious gatherings antedates the medieval cathedral, reaching back to the synagogue tradition of the first century or earlier. The early synagogue, however, must have been a far less reverberant space than the medieval cathedral, because it was used for sermons and scriptural readings. The fact that the medieval cathedral emphasized music and visual splendor rather than speech can be seen both as a change from the earlier synagogue practice, and as an appropriate adaptation to the new acoustical environment of the cathedral. Medieval experimenters must have searched for ways to reduce the interference of reverberation with the verbal liturgy. Gregorian chant and polyphonic music may be among the fruits of this search.

Using the terms of modern communications theory, the reverberant acoustical environment of a cathedral may be described as a "time-dispersive communications channel," wherein a talker's short utterance (word or syllable) persists at the listener's ears for a period of time that may be long compared to the duration of the utterance. Because of this time-dispersion, words uttered in rapid sequence are heard simultaneously, thus interfering with one another and causing confusion for the listener.

The interference can be reduced somewhat by speaking slowly, leaving spaces between utterances so that the previous utterance is permitted to decay before the next one is received. The slow and stately chant of cathedral liturgy is a practical application of this ancient discovery. Modern communication theory recognizes that the strategy of reducing speech rate has merit for coping with reverberation, but at the cost of a very low rate of verbal information transmission.

A more subtle way to increase the verbal information transmission rate is to employ *singing* instead of speech. Singing exploits the frequency selectivity of human hearing. This property of hearing permits simultaneous reception without interference of sounds that are separated in frequency. For example, syllables sung consecutively at different pitch in a cathedral are heard simultaneously because of reverberation, but may be intelligible nevertheless if the ear can resolve their separation in frequency. This prescription for efficient verbal communication in a reverberant environment begins to describe the *syllabic style* of Gregorian chant. Modern communication theory would recognize this medieval strategy as a form of "frequency diversity transmission," that is often used for increasing the low rate of information transmission in time-dispersive communication channels such as these.

Since two or more voices are heard simultaneously when chant is sung in a cathedral, all musical consonances and dissonances are much more striking than they would be in a less reverberant space. Therefore, the need to render chant artful, as well as efficient, must have drawn increased attention to the rules of harmony. Thus did cathedral acoustics perhaps hasten the development of polyphony and harmony in western music.

While high speech intelligibility was not required in the medieval cathedral, it has become a common requirement since the Reformation. The Reformation began a period of liturgical reform that placed more emphasis on "the word," and consequently, the necessity for high speech intelligibility. An acoustical expression of that reform is seen in the tendency to design much lower reverberation time into post-Reformation worship spaces. The two-second mid-frequency reverberation time (occupied) of J. S. Bach's Thomas-Kirche is but a fraction of that found in great medieval cathedrals (about 10–12 seconds). Even lower reverberation time (below one second, occupied) is to be found in the small New England Meeting House, which seems much better adapted to speech than to traditional sacred music. For large traditional worship spaces this period of reform is still current, as testified by the actions of the Second Vatican Council which mandates that great care be taken in church architecture to ensure "... the active participation of the faithful."

Since music and sermon alternate in the liturgy, worship spaces must be suitable for both. Traditional music is not entirely discarded even if it no longer quite fits modern conditions. New music and services continue to be written, adapting current technology and liturgy to express denominational and congregational style. Electronics, the revolutionary technology of our age, is an element of that adaptation.

Electronic Augmentation of Worship Space Acoustics

Electronic sound systems are brought into worship spaces to resolve the conflicting acoustical need described above, with mixed results. In worship spaces having long reverberation time, speech reinforcement systems are often used in an effort to render "the word" intelligible. This is a challenging task fraught with peril. Advances in electronic art are gradually improving the record of success of speech reinforcement systems. Examples of this are included in the Poster Papers. Another growing trend is the use of special electronic assistive listening systems for the hearing impaired. A brief essay on that subject is also included.

Worship spaces having short reverberation time more suited to speech are subject to acoustical problems related to music performance attendant on the loss of reverberation. Examples of this are also found in this book. In these relatively "dead" spaces, choir members may not hear one another well enough to produce artful song. Congregational singing, too, may suffer from both poor coordination, and "dead" sound. Musical instruments may sound feeble without the sound amplifying assistance of reverberation, especially toward the rear of larger worship spaces. Here, a larger organ may be required—but may not always be feasible—to compensate for the loss of reverberation. Electronics is sometimes used to amplify the organ and other instruments in an acoustically "dead" worship space such as these. An advantage of using acoustically dead spaces is that the sound is can be varied as the occasion requires. In such rooms the amount and quality of sound is determined "actively" by the sound system rather than "passively" by the architectural acoustics. As discussed in David Klepper's essay, gradually such worship spaces have begun to resemble sound studios. In some cases, the audio requirements actually resemble those of night clubs or rock music concerts.

The Electronic Church

A recent trend toward "electronic ministries" especially among evangelical churches makes use of electronic sound to a degree unprecedented in the history of worship space acoustics. These churches have literally become sound and video studios, broadcasting worship services to their community, or even to the world through satellite link. The sound requirements here are those of broadcast studios and musical theatre, the "sound man" is king, and passive interior acoustics are of diminished importance. Evangelical churches are in the vanguard of institutions adapting new electronic technology and music to worship.

Every congregation can expect to have individuals with special hearing needs for speech that will be overlooked in the conventional acoustical design of a worship space. Addressing these special needs takes patience, persistence, understanding, and budget, but can increase the participation, understanding, and joy of the hearing handicapped. It would be difficult to overestimate the contribution this could make to the life and spirit of these individuals, many of whom suffer terrible social isolation. But, these special hearing needs can only be addressed if their requirements are identified and incorporated into the building plan. As first steps toward developing such a plan, we need to ask: Who are these people? How many are in my congregation? What are their special hearing needs? How can they be accommodated? For this purpose, Anna Nabelek offers her insights, gained through research experience in the measurement of indoor speech intelligibility for various categories of listener.

Accommodating Listeners with Special Needs in Worship Spaces

Anna K. Nabelek, Ph.D.
Department of Audiology and Speech Pathology
The University of Tennessee
Knoxville, TN 37996

Categories of Listeners with Special Needs

Who are the listeners with special needs? They are first of all people with hearing impairment. Many of the hearing-impaired can understand speech only in quiet environments and refuse to use their personal hearing aids in noisy places. Others do not wear hearing aids and understand speech only when it is shouted.

In addition to hearing-impaired people, the elderly, even those with quite good hearing, exhibit less tolerance to noise and reverberation. This low tolerance to noise and reverberation seems to be one of the manifestations of aging of the hearing mechanism. It is also found that young children, 10 years of age and less, tend to hear worse in adverse listening conditions than young adults. It is believed that young children have less developed listening skills than adults and cannot concentrate well on the spoken words.

There is evidence that non-native listeners are less proficient at understanding speech contaminated by noise and reverberation than are native listeners. This finding seems striking because many non-native listeners who were studied were able to comprehend English words very well in a quiet and nonreverberant environment, and many were proficient in English.

Demographics of Hearing Impairment

According to data from the National Health Survey published in 1982 by the U.S. Department of Health and Human Services, 7% of the population have some trouble hearing speech indoors and 4% report such great difficulty that only shouted speech can be partially understood. The percentage of the population with hearing problems changes with age. Elderly people have more hearing problems than do young adults. According to the same statistical source, 26% of people 65 years of age and over have some hearing problems and 16% of those at best can hear shouted speech.

These demographics indicate that a sizable percentage of members of each congregation will have some hearing loss. Such people need higher sound pressure levels than those with normal hearing to perceive sounds and especially to understand spoken words. One might assume that people with substantial hearing problems wear hearing aids which provide adequate amplification for each individual. However, according to the same above mentioned statistic, only 1/3 of the people who report that they, at best, can hear shouted speech wear hearing aids. What are the chances of the remaining 2/3 to understand spoken words in worship spaces? Some congregations provide interpreters who use sign language to help the deaf. However, many hard-of-hearing people do not use sign language, choosing to rely on house amplification.

The Uses of Assistive Listening Systems

Many worship spaces use house public address systems that are designed to proved uniform speech sound pressure levels over the whole congregation seating area. The amplified sound levels may be correct for normal listeners, but too low for people with substantial hearing loss. Of course it is impractical to increase amplification for everyone in order to suit the most severely impaired listeners. What can be done for these people? First, they can be encouraged to sit in front pews, since conditions for listening and lip-reading are usually more favorable there. If this is not enough, they can be helped with individual amplification provided by so-called *assistive listening systems.*

Assistive listening systems can be distinguished from public address systems by the way in which sound is delivered to the listeners. While public address systems deliver sound to a group through one or more loudspeakers, assistive listening systems deliver sound to individuals through headphones, or through a device that connects to their personal hearing aid.

For the listener with special hearing needs, there are two major advantages of assistive listening systems over public address systems:

(1) sound can be individually amplified to the desired level;
(2) sound is free from background noise and room reverberation.

These advantages are realized by transmitting sounds electronically from the microphone to the listener instead of by acoustic waves in air, as in the case of the loudspeaker. Three means of transmission in current use for assistive listening systems are

(1) induction magnetic field (associated with so-called induction loops)
(2) electromagnetic waves in radio transmitting systems (AM and FM systems), and
(3) invisible light waves used in infrared systems.

Research studies indicate that for many hearing-impaired listeners (and also for some others who have listening difficulties but otherwise normal hearing, such as the elderly and foreigners), speech should contain very little reverberation and background noise to be fully understandable. It has been shown that speech should be at least 10 decibels (dB) above the background noise level and reverberation time should not exceed one-half second to allow the special listeners to achieve the best possible speech discrimination.

Such conditions might be difficult to achieve in many worship spaces. While background noise is ordinarily low, the mixing of music with spoken words can cause problems for the special listeners. The reverberation time is ordinarily longer than one-half second, and this degrades speech intelligibility for hearing handicapped listeners.

In summary, *every* congregation can expect to have a substantial percentage of listeners who possess below-normal listening skills or abilities. These listeners can be helped considerably by well-designed acoustics and by the use of special assistive listening systems.

The Use of Acoustical Consultants for Worship Space Projects

Most of the projects reported in this book were done with the help of acoustical consultants.

An experienced acoustical consultant can contribute substantially to the goal of obtaining excellent acoustics in a worship space. By *composing* good questions, *proposing* good solutions and compromises, and *exposing* bad ones, a good consultant can save more money than he costs. If brought into a project at its origin and made aware of its objectives, an experienced consultant can help to establish the criteria necessary for its physical realization. Too often, an acoustical consultant is brought into a project too late, after a problem is recognized. By then, the damage may be done, and the consultant's contribution may be limited to suggesting how to make the best of a bad situation.

Below is a sample list of ten areas in which an acoustical consultant may contribute to the excellence of a worship space project:

1. Site selection studies (present and future environmental noise due to vehicular traffic, aircraft, construction noise).
2. Interior acoustic criteria (room noise and speech intelligibility criteria, reverberation time).
3. Interior design considerations (location and shape of choir area, pulpit, organ rehearsal facilities, classrooms, machinery).
4. Interior material selection and measurement (pew benches and cushions, draperies, wall and ceiling finishes).
5. Sound system design (loudspeaker locations, microphones, delay units, assistive listening systems).
6. Mechanical system noise and vibration control (HVAC, plumbing, etc.).
7. Control of sound transmission from adjacent spaces and exterior noise sources.
8. Review of work performed by architects and interior designers.
9. Measurement and evaluation of acoustics for speech and/or music.
10. Corrective recommendations for completed buildings.

Acoustical consultants may be retained by the building's owners or their representatives (e.g., a "building committee"), or by the architect.

The nontrivial question of how to find and retain a good acoustical consultant deserves some attention. Sometimes a consultant is chosen by reputation, or on the recommendation of an architect or another past client. Lacking a trusted source of referral, one may search through the directory of National Council of Acoustical Consultants.

The National Council of Acoustical Consultants

Many acoustical consultants are members of the National Council of Acoustical Consultants (NCAC), an association of acoustical consulting firms that have "demonstrated capabilities and expertise in the field of acoustics." Criteria for Membership in the NCAC includes full Membership in the Acoustical Society of America (the primary scientific society for professionals in the field of acoustics), knowledge and training in acoustics, experience in acoustical consulting, subscription to a canon of ethics, and business qualifications, including the ability to provide independent and unbiased advice to the public.

The NCAC also cooperates and maintains close liaison with the Institute of Noise Control Engineers (INCE), the American Consulting Engineers Council (ACEC), the National Society of Professional Engineers (NSPE), and other organizations.

The NCAC publishes a Membership Directory listing the names and interests of Member firms. Many of these firms are interested and qualified to practice in worship space acoustics. Although some non-member firms may also have excellent qualifications to practice in this field, the NCAC Directory is the only list of its kind. Currently, the NCAC Directory can be obtained for $1 by referring to this book and writing to

NCAC
66 Morris Avenue
Springfield, NJ 07081

Included in the NCAC Directory is advice on the important task of selecting an acoustical consultant. It is reproduced below.

Selection of an Acoustical Consultant

Every project undertaken by an acoustical consultant is unique. While many assignments may be similar in nature, no two ever are identical. For this reason, it is essential that a consultant be chosen with deliberate care. In essence, the more experienced and qualified he is to undertake a given project, the more likely his services will be in accord with the goals and objectives of his client. Moreover, provision of consulting services, by definition, implies a close, privileged relationship between the consultant and his client. To give less than full consideration to the selection/retention process, therefore, would be to jeopardize a successful consultant–client relationship before it begins, thereby jeopardizing the successful outcome of the project at hand.

In the event that you have not already established a relationship with an acoustical consultant, the National Council of Acoustical Consultants recommends for your consideration the following method of selection and retention, tested through many years of successful application.

1. Determine to the extent possible the nature and scope of the problem or assignment involved.
2. Through contact with mutual acquaintances who have previously utilized acoustical consultants, or from directories of qualified independent consulting firms provided by an organization such as NCAC, identify one or more acoustical consultants who, by virtue of previous experience, stated capabilities, availability and proximity of location, as well as other relevant factors, appear to be generally qualified to undertake the project.
3. Provide project details to the consultants so identified and request from each statements of qualification, including a complete description of the firm, previous assignments and clients, names and biographies of persons who would be working on the project, anticipated time schedules involved, and other factors that relate to the quality of work to be performed.
4. After thorough review of applicant firms' credentials and experience data, possibly including direct contact with firm representatives if such can be arranged, identify the firm that appears most qualifed to serve your specific requirements.
5. Contact representatives of that firm felt to be most qualified and open negotiations to establish a mutually acceptable consulting fee arrangement and payment methodology. Most consultants are experienced in at least several types of retention agreements, including hourly rate, fixed fee, cost plus fixed fee, percentage of overhead, etc. Usually one of these will be most suited to the type of work involved.
6. If the negotiations prove satisfactory, the client should at this point retain the consultant to ensure his availability for the project. If negotiations are not successful, they should be terminated and opened with other qualified firms, one at a time.

It should be noted that NCAC encourages open and frank discussion of financial concerns between the client and consultant. Experience demonstrates that mutually satisfactory client–consultant relationships rest predominantly on the consultant's ability to deliver cost-effective services on time and within the scope of the agreement. In fact, most successful consultants pride themselves on their ability to tailor their efforts to the scope of the project and the budget available for services as well as for implementation of the recommendations resulting from their services. It is urged strongly, however, that discussions of fees be divorced completely from the ranking of qualifications to prevent financial considerations from biasing the selection process. True economy results only when services provided are cost-effective in the long term, helping ensure results that satisfy the client's needs from an overall standpoint. A consultant who is fully competent to undertake the work is the one most likely to provide such results.

SUMMARY OF WORSHIP SPACES

WHITESBURG BAPTIST CHURCH
HUNTSVILLE, ALABAMA

COMPLETED: 1982

ARCHITECT: Jones & Herrin
                                  Atlanta, Georgia

ACOUSTICAL CONSULTANT: Purcell & Noppe & Assoc., Inc.
                                  Chatsworth, California
                                  Roger C. Noppe, Partner in
                                       Charge

COST: $5,000,000

The recently completed auditorium for the Whitesburg Baptist Church, Huntsville, Alabama, was designed and constructed to meet the needs of a rapidly growing congregation committed to an active contemporary gospel music program. A radio ministry and a soon-to-be initiated television ministry also were important considerations.

The Pastor, Minister of Music, and members of the Building Committee toured a number of contemporary auditoria and church facilities, and selected the Grand Ole Opry Auditorium in Nashville, Tennessee (also a P&N&A project) as the facility which best met their acoustical design objectives.

The Whitesburg Baptist Church auditorium has a planned seating capacity of 3000, temporarily reduced to 2400 by partitions which close off the underbalcony area - at present utilized as classroom space. The wide "fan plan" was selected by the architects to minimize the distance between congregation members and the choir/pulpit/lectern locations.

In order to achieve the above acoustical objectives, the auditorium was designed to a mid-frequency reverberation time of 1.8 to 1.9 seconds and a maximum ambient noise level due to building equipment of NC-25.

Electroacoustics play an important part in the successful utilization of the space. The systems designed by P&N&A include a highly directional monophonic cluster of loudspeakers for speech and soloists, positioned at the center line of the auditorium (above the lectern and pulpit location), together with a three channel stereophonic choir reinforcement system, a pulpit-to-choir speech reinforcement system, and a choir "cross mix" system which provides a foldback to the choir members to assist in ensemble.

WHITESBURG BAPTIST CHURCH
HUNTSVILLE, ALABAMA
1982

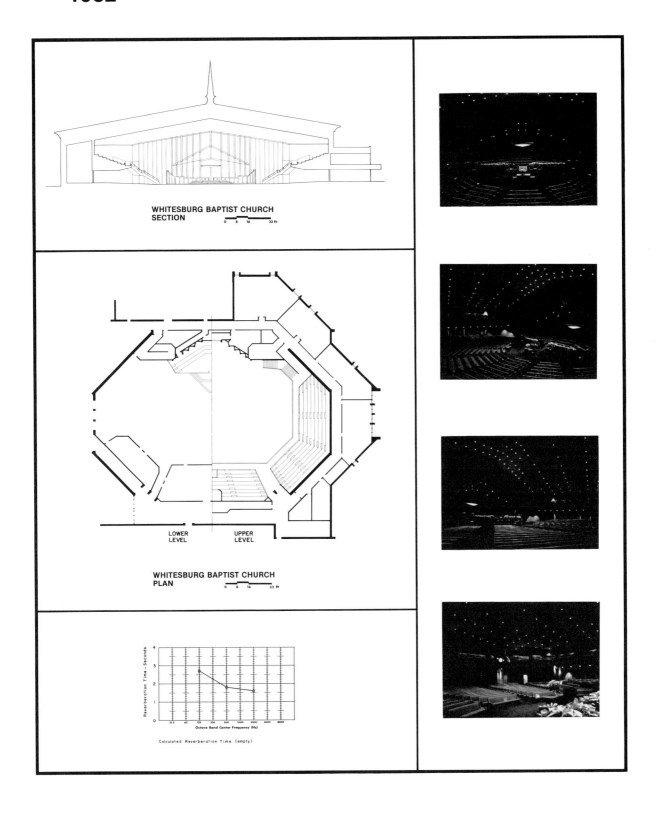

WHITESBURG BAPTIST CHURCH
SECTION

0   8   16   32 ft

LOWER
LEVEL

UPPER
LEVEL

WHITESBURG BAPTIST CHURCH
PLAN

0   8   16   32 ft

Reverberation Time—Seconds

31.3   63   125   250   500   1000   2000   4000   8000
Octave Band Center Frequency (Hz)

Calculated Reverberation Time (empty)

GRAND AVENUE BAPTIST CHURCH
FORT SMITH, ARKANSAS

COMPLETED:	1981
ARCHITECT:	Laser, Knight, Hathaway & Guest Fort Smith, Arkansas
ACOUSTICAL CONSULTANT:	Joiner-Pelton-Rose, Inc. Dallas, Texas

The Grand Avenue Baptist Church, with a seating capacity of 2100, required a 120-degree, fan-shaped design to meet the architect's design goal of keeping all seats within 66 feet of the services. This arrangement allows good sight and sound characteristics, while maintaining a feeling of intimacy and involvement.

A key acoustic criterion was the control of focused reflections from the curved rear wall and balcony face. Absorptive materials were placed on the critical surfaces to ensure that design goals were met.

A central speaker cluster, located in an enclosure integrated into the ceiling over the chancel platform, is augmented by time-delayed ceiling speakers under the deep balcony overhang. Mechanical noise control measures were implemented to meet the NC25 - 30 design criteria. A floating floor was required because a conference room is located under the HVAC equipment. At the request of the church, room response was purposely designed with little reverberation to favor speech intelligibility.

GRAND AVENUE BAPTIST CHURCH
FT. SMITH, ARKANSAS
COMPLETED 1981

JOINER-PELTON-ROSE, INC

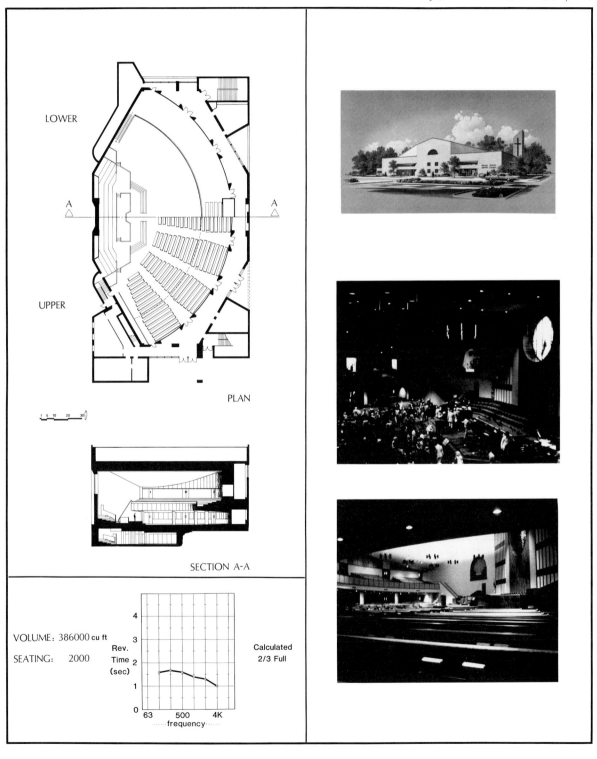

LOWER

A
A

UPPER

PLAN

1 5 10   20   30

SECTION A-A

VOLUME: 386000 cu ft

SEATING: 2000

Rev.
Time
(sec)

Calculated
2/3 Full

4
3
2
1
0

63   500   4K

frequency

HOPE LUTHERAN CHURCH
DALY CITY, CALIFORNIA

COMPLETED:	1955
EVALUATED:	1983
ARCHITECT:	Mario Corbett AIA Associates San Francisco, California
ACOUSTICAL CONSULTANT:	Paoletti/Lewitz/Associates Inc. San Francisco, California

Church organizations, such as Hope Lutheran, often seek the assistance of an acoustical consultant to evaluate and improve their existing facilities. Our analysis and measurements showed that a number of key factors contributed to the generally poor acoustical quality of the sanctuary.

The existing sound reinforcement system, even though very basic, was not being used properly. We recommended a longer gooseneck so that the lectern microphone would be closer to the speaker's mouth to improve sound pickup. Loudspeakers mounted along the sides of the sloped roof beam were aimed straight down the side walls. We recommended reorienting them approximately 25 degrees towards the audience to increase the loudspeaker coverage for listeners.

The cross-shaped glass design on the building facade faces a major freeway, a few hundred feet away. Noise from automobile tires penetrates the building facade. Air leaks from the chest and blower pipe of the old organ also contribute to high background sound in the sanctuary. Low frequency noise from the main organ blower is not adequately isolated. These sources of noise detract from the desired quiet interior environment for speech and music.

At high frequencies there are significant losses of sound energy within the sanctuary. These include sound absorption from carpeting throughout the altar area; sound absorption through the gaps between the roof-deck planks; the roof timbers protruding into the space that obstruct clear sound reflection from choir to congregation: and poor sound projection from the choir located off-center and on the flat floor of the choir loft.

This relatively small project illustrates the many simple observations and recommendations which may be obvious to an acoustical consultant and can lead to a much improved acoustical environment.

HOPE LUTHERAN CHURCH
DALY CITY, CALIFORNIA USA
COMPLETED 1955, EVALUATED 1983

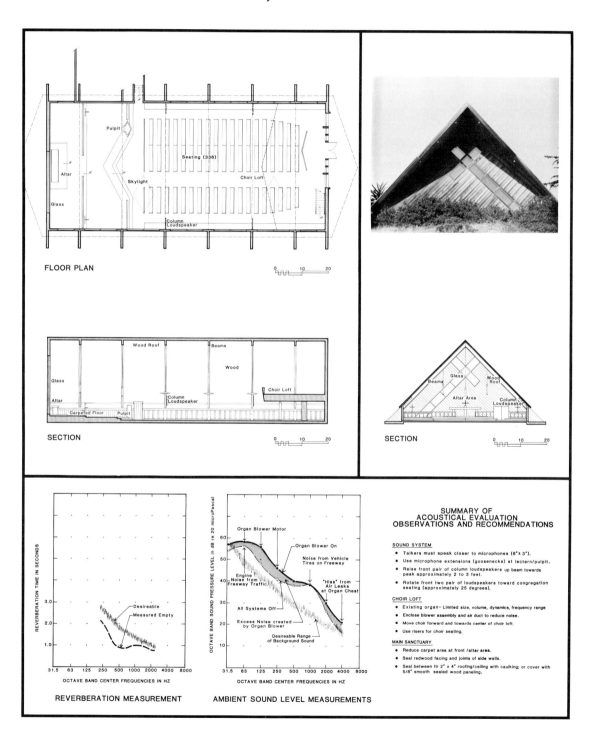

FLOOR PLAN

0   10   20

SECTION

0   10   20

SECTION

0   10   20

REVERBERATION MEASUREMENT

AMBIENT SOUND LEVEL MEASUREMENTS

SUMMARY OF
ACOUSTICAL EVALUATION
OBSERVATIONS AND RECOMMENDATIONS

SOUND SYSTEM

- Talkers must speak closer to microphones (6" ± 3").
- Use microphone extensions (goosenecks) at lectern/pulpit.
- Raise front pair of column loudspeakers up beam towards peak approximately 2 to 3 feet.
- Rotate front two pair of loudspeakers toward congregation seating (approximately 25 degrees).

CHOIR LOFT

- Existing organ– Limited size, volume, dynamics, frequency range
- Enclose blower assembly and air duct to reduce noise.
- Move choir forward and towards center of choir loft.
- Use risers for choir seating.

MAIN SANCTUARY

- Reduce carpet area at front /altar area.
- Seal redwood facing and joints of side walls.
- Seal between fir 2" x 4" roofing/ceiling with caulking; or cover with 5/8" smooth sealed wood paneling.

COMMUNITY PRESBYTERIAN CHURCH
DANVILLE, CALIFORNIA

COMPLETED: June 1979

ARCHITECT: E. Paul Kelly, Architect
                                        Berkeley, California

ACOUSTICAL CONSULTANT: Paoletti/Lewitz/Associates Inc.
                                        San Francisco, California

ELECTRICAL ENGINEER: T. H. Rogers & Associates
                                        Berkeley, California

MECHANICAL ENGINEER: Montgomery & Roberts
                                        Oakland, California

The architect has designed a number of churches in the Bay Area, including the 700 seat Community Presbyterian Church. A unique consideration of this particular church was its flexibility in providing the congregation with a space that was suitable for both worship and community activities. The sound system design had to accommodate this flexibility as well as the physical and acoustical needs of the space itself.

The church design required three separate platform locations from which the service and other programs could be conducted. This necessitated a flexible sound system design which consists of 31 distributed 8″ diameter, ceiling-mounted loudspeakers. The size and nature of the programs, many of which involve musical performances, required a digital audio delay for the loudspeaker system. A custom switching matrix automatically assigns the proper audio delay to each loudspeaker for each platform location.

Each platform location is provided with receptacles for microphones and monitor loudspeakers. The microphone receptacles connect to a jack field in the sound control position at the rear of the church. From this position, the operator can see and hear the same mixture of live and reinforced sound as the congregation.

The sound amplification system also includes a hard-of-hearing amplification system and monitor loudspeakers in ancillary spaces. The ceiling loudspeakers are mounted in enclosures which visually complement the lighting fixtures. The performance of the sound system has answered the needs for high quality speech reinforcement and music playback.

COMMUNITY PRESBYTERIAN CHURCH
DANVILLE, CALIFORNIA USA
COMPLETED 1979

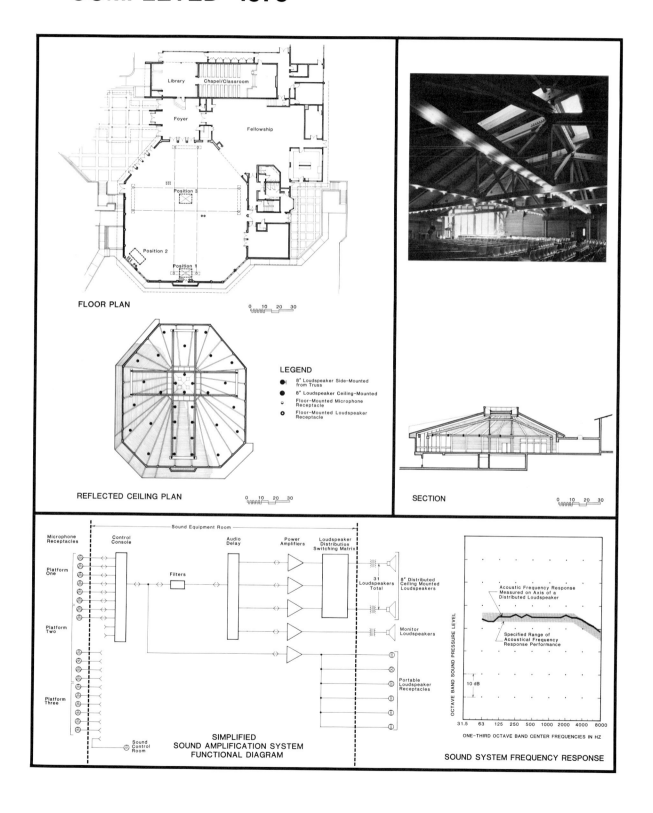

FLOOR PLAN

0 10 20 30

REFLECTED CEILING PLAN

0 10 20 30

LEGEND

- 8" Loudspeaker Side-Mounted from Truss
- 8" Loudspeaker Ceiling-Mounted
- Floor-Mounted Microphone Receptacle
- Floor-Mounted Loudspeaker Receptacle

SECTION

0 10 20 30

SIMPLIFIED
SOUND AMPLIFICATION SYSTEM
FUNCTIONAL DIAGRAM

SOUND SYSTEM FREQUENCY RESPONSE

BETHEL OPEN BIBLE CHURCH
LODI, CALIFORNIA

CONSTRUCTED: 1982

ARCHITECT: Morris and Wenell
                                       Lodi, California

ACOUSTICAL CONSULTANT: Arthur K. Yeap & ADI Group
                                       San Francisco, California

STRUCTURAL ENGINEER: Arthur E. Ross Inc.
                                       Sacramento, California

COST: $1,500,000

This sanctuary design is representative of a new generation of evangelical worship spaces. A desire for better visibility and greater intimacy with the speaker and platform is provided by fan-shaped seating with liberal usage of lighter colors and natural wood. Piano, mixed choir and congregational worship are the principal forms of music, with frequent usage of drama, orchestra and amplified contemporary music.

The architect included portions of an existing structure with newer portions constructed of concrete block and rock. The remainder of the building is wood frame with gypsum board and plywood. The front and back walls include wood slatting and the steel shell is incorporated into the platform design. The whole sanctuary is carpeted and the seats are heavily upholstered. Absorptive treatment of fabric and wool was placed on the wood walls with the wood slats dampened to removed a perceived brightness in the upper mid frequencies. The sound operator's booth has been placed in an ideal location in the middle of the seating area.

The sound system was designed for maximum fidelity and clarity. Coverage is extremely even at any point and the lack of feedback is quite remarkable. Maximum SPL at the rear has been measured at 119 dB. An in-house designed central array utilizing very linear drivers and bi-radial horns has been installed with great detail placed on phase and crossover design for the triamped system. Comprehensive recording and patching facilities have been provided along with the 24 channel mixer.

The room has achieved a very neutral sound and has been described as being "very intimate" without being too dry, probably attributed to the dispersive ceiling elements along with the absorptive sidewalls. The sound system has been highly praised by both artist and listener alike.

bethel open bible church
lodi, california
1982

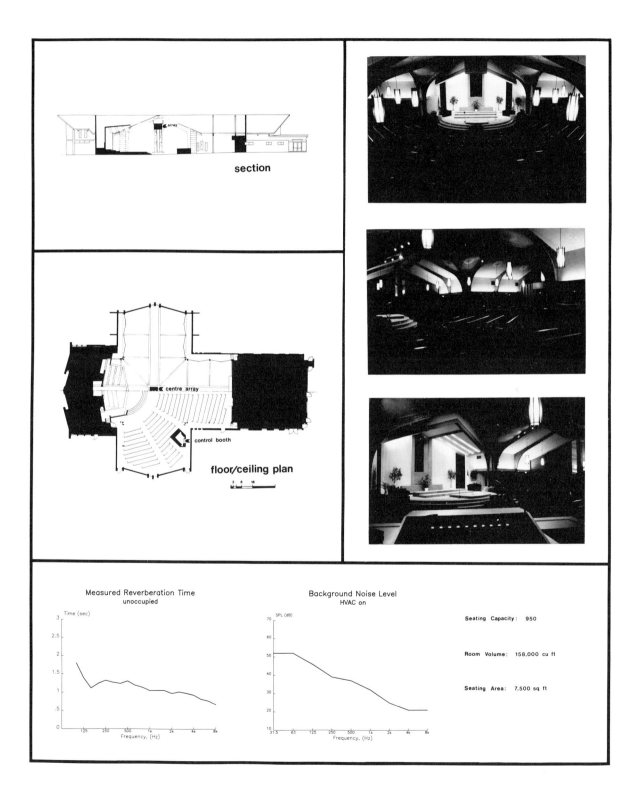

section

centre array

control booth

floor/ceiling plan

Measured Reverberation Time
unoccupied

Time (sec)

Frequency, (Hz)

Background Noise Level
HVAC on

SPL (dB)

Frequency, (Hz)

Seating Capacity: 950

Room Volume: 158,000 cu ft

Seating Area: 7,500 sq ft

GRACE BRETHREN CHURCH
LONG BEACH, CALIFORNIA

COMPLETED: 1967

OWNER: Grace Brethren Church, Inc.

ARCHITECT: Richard L. Poper and
                                    Jess J. Jones

STRUCTURAL ENGINEER: Charley C. Curtis

ELECTRICAL ENGINEER: H. Simmons

MECHANICAL ENGINEER: Kenneth G. Ambrose

ACOUSTICAL CONSULTANT: Ludwig W. Sepmeyer

COST: $895,000

Acoustical Design Features:

To cover both the main floor and the balcony with natural sound, without echoes, and to achieve a balanced compromise in the reverberation time between speech and organ music.

GRACE BRETHREN CHURCH
LONG BEACH, CA
1967

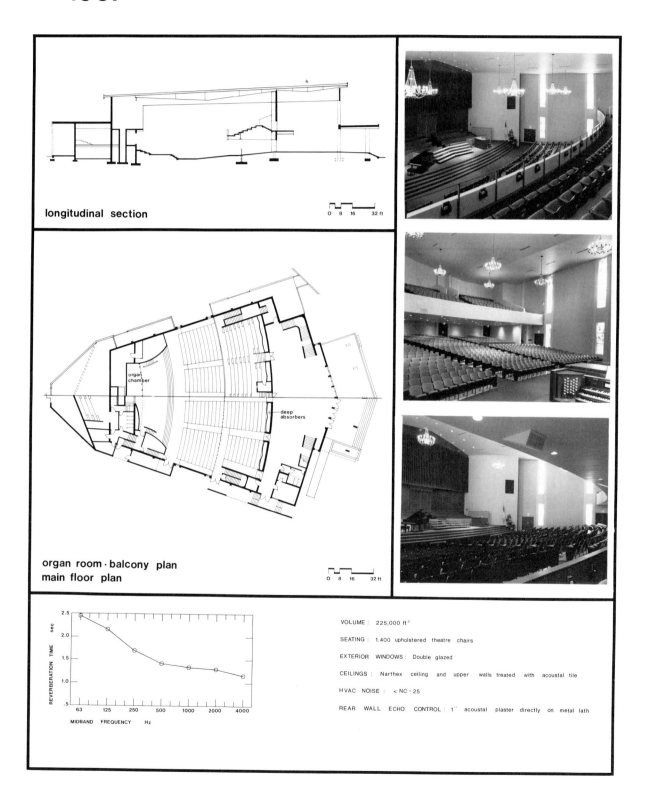

longitudinal section

0   8   16   32 ft

organ
chamber

deep
absorbers

organ room · balcony plan
main floor plan

0   8   16   32 ft

REVERBERATION TIME   sec

2.5
2.0
1.5
1.0
.5

63   125   250   500   1000   2000   4000

MIDBAND   FREQUENCY   Hz

VOLUME :   225,000 ft³

SEATING :   1.400 upholstered theatre chairs

EXTERIOR WINDOWS :   Double glazed

CEILINGS :   Narthex ceiling and upper walls treated with acoustal tile

HVAC NOISE :   < NC - 25

REAR WALL ECHO CONTROL : 1″ acoustal plaster directly on metal lath

GRACE BRETHREN CHAPEL
LONG BEACH, CALIFORNIA

COMPLETED: 1967

OWNER: Grace Brethren Church, Inc.

ARCHITECT: Richard L. Poper and
                                    Jess J. Jones

STRUCTURAL ENGINEER: Charley C. Curtis

ELECTRICAL ENGINEER: H. Simmons

MECHANICAL ENGINEER: Kenneth G. Ambrose

ACOUSTICAL CONSULTANT: Ludwig W. Sepmeyer

CHAPEL COSTS: $204,000

Acoustical Design Features:

Simply to achieve a pleasant, comfortable area for worship.

GRACE BRETHREN CHAPEL
LONG BEACH, CA
1967

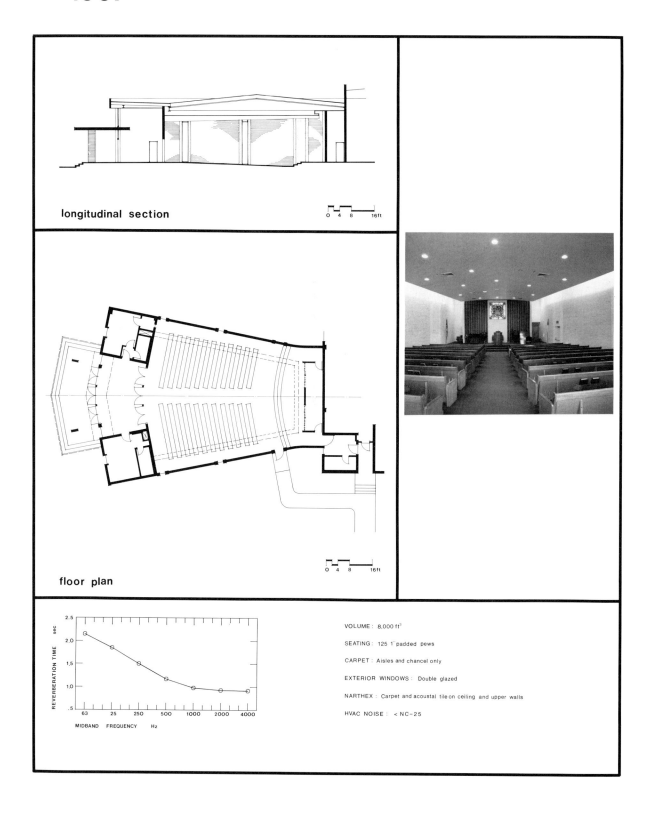

longitudinal section

0 4 8   16ft

floor plan

0 4 8   16ft

REVERBERATION TIME   sec

2.5

2.0

1.5

1.0

.5

63   25   250   500   1000   2000   4000

MIDBAND   FREQUENCY   Hz

VOLUME : 8,000 ft³

SEATING : 125 1' padded pews

CARPET : Aisles and chancel only

EXTERIOR WINDOWS : Double glazed

NARTHEX : Carpet and acoustal tile on ceiling and upper walls

HVAC NOISE : < NC-25

HERRICK MEMORIAL CHAPEL
OCCIDENTAL COLLEGE
LOS ANGELES, CALIFORNIA

COMPLETED: 1964

OWNER: Occidental College

ARCHITECT: Ladd and Kelsey
                                        Pasadena, California

ACOUSTICAL CONSULTANT: Bolt Beranek and Newman Inc.
                                        Canoga Park, California

The chapel was a gift to Occidental College from John Pierce Herrick in honor of his wife, Margaret Brown Herrick. The cruciform plan is formed from eight free-standing reinforced concrete units capped by the roof and central dome.

The chapel has 580 seats and accommodates any type of Christian liturgical worship, in addition to a wide range of musical programs. The lower level contains a social lounge, offices and seminar rooms.

The stained glass was designed and fabricated by Perli Pelzig in his Los Angeles studios. Most of the stained glass was imported from Europe. The dominant windows develop Christian themes chosen for areas of the liberal arts.

The 60 rank, 3 manual chapel organ was built by the Schlicker Organ Company of Buffalo, N.Y. It is in two sections, one on either side of the west window, and is enclosed within walls of loudspeaker grille cloth.

The acoustical design of the chapel is based on optimum performance of liturgical works, with a speech reinforcement system utilizing highly-directional horn loudspeakers located above the ceiling plane. Comments from organists and other musicians concerning the acoustics have been generally very favorable.

HERRICK MEMORIAL CHAPEL
OCCIDENTAL COLLEGE, LOS ANGELES
COMPLETED 1964

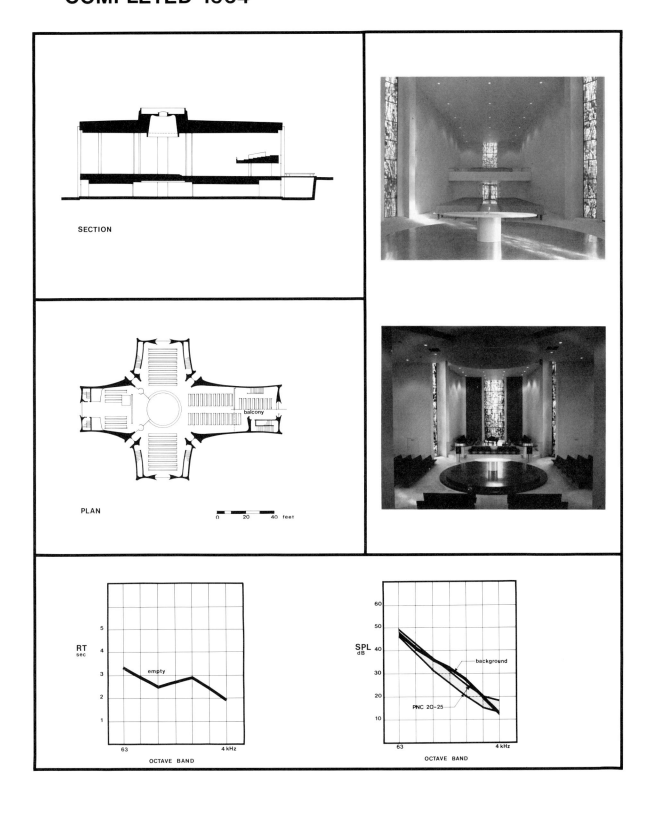

SECTION

PLAN

0   20   40 feet

RT
sec

empty

OCTAVE BAND

63   4 kHz

SPL
dB

background

PNC 20-25

OCTAVE BAND

63   4 kHz

ST. BASIL'S CATHOLIC CHURCH
LOS ANGELES, CALIFORNIA

COMPLETED: 1969

OWNER: Archdiocese of Los Angeles

ARCHITECT: Albert C. Martin & Associates
                                    Los Angeles, California

ACOUSTICAL CONSULTANT: Bolt Beranek and Newman Inc.
                                    Canoga Park, California

St. Basil's Catholic Church replaced an earlier wood frame building, which was destroyed by fire six months before the dedication of the new building in 1969. The architectural design reflects the inspiration of a third-century Roman church, utilizing poured concrete walls punctuated by tall, slender stained-glass windows, with ornamental elements of wood.

The three-dimensional sculptural stained-glass windows, designed by Claire Falkenstein, provide a rich contrast to the simplicity and massiveness of the concrete walls. A free-standing balcony over the narthex accommodates the choir and a 32 rank, 3 manual organ by Justin Kramer of Los Angeles.

Because of its height—74 feet—and construction the sanctuary is highly reverberant, providing rich enhancement of musical events. Speech reinforcement is provided via a cluster of highly-directional horn loudspeakers located directly above the pulpit. When the person speaking is close to the microphone, speech intelligibility is quite adequate in most locations.

ST. BASIL'S CATHOLIC CHURCH
LOS ANGELES
COMPLETED 1969

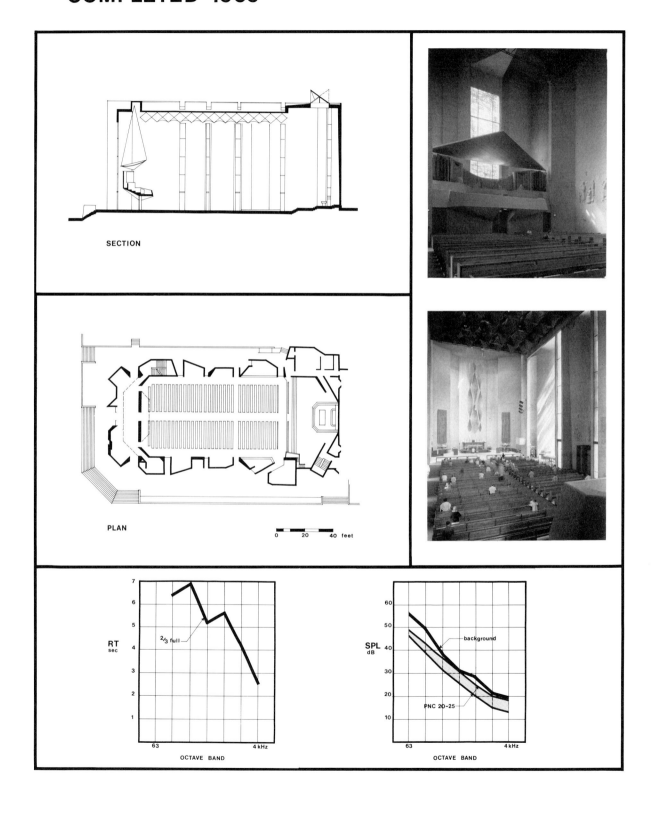

SECTION

PLAN

0   20   40 feet

RT
sec

⅔ full

63   4 kHz

OCTAVE BAND

SPL
dB

background

PNC 20-25

63   4 kHz

OCTAVE BAND

BETH EDEN BAPTIST CHURCH
OAKLAND, CALIFORNIA

COMPLETED:	April 1982
ARCHITECT:	E. Paul Kelly, Berkeley, Calif.
ACOUSTICAL CONSULTANT:	Paoletti/Lewitz/Associates Inc. San Francisco, California
STRUCTURAL ENGINEER:	S. J. Medwadowski San Francisco, California
MECHANICAL ENGINEER:	T&T Enterprises Oakland, California
ELECTRICAL ENGINEER:	WHM Inc., Orinda, California

Architect Paul Kelly provided a visually pleasing space utilizing wood and glass as the principal construction materials. The church seats 700 on the main floor and 150 in the balcony. The use of carpet and upholstered pews provides control of reverberation and sound energy is directed toward the seating areas from the distributed, ceiling mounted loudspeakers.

The worship service includes highly amplified musical performances with instruments as well as a large gospel choir. Properly shaped and oriented sound reflecting surfaces at the altar and above the choir provide a mixture of live and reinforced sound for all members of the congregation, thus achieving naturalness and directional realism in the space.

The sound amplification system includes: microphones for speech reinforcement, amplification of instruments and choir reinforcement. The choir microphone system includes suspended PZM microphones which provide uniform pickup of the choir members. The system also includes monitoring loudspeakers for ancillary spaces, including church offices and lobbies.

The ability for participants on the platform to hear each other adequately was a prime consideration in the design of the sound amplification system. Therefore, stage monitoring and monitor sound mix was provided.

A sound control booth overlooking the sanctuary contains the sound control mixing console and the equipment racks housing the system electronics.

BETH EDEN BAPTIST CHURCH
OAKLAND, CALIFORNIA USA
COMPLETED 1982

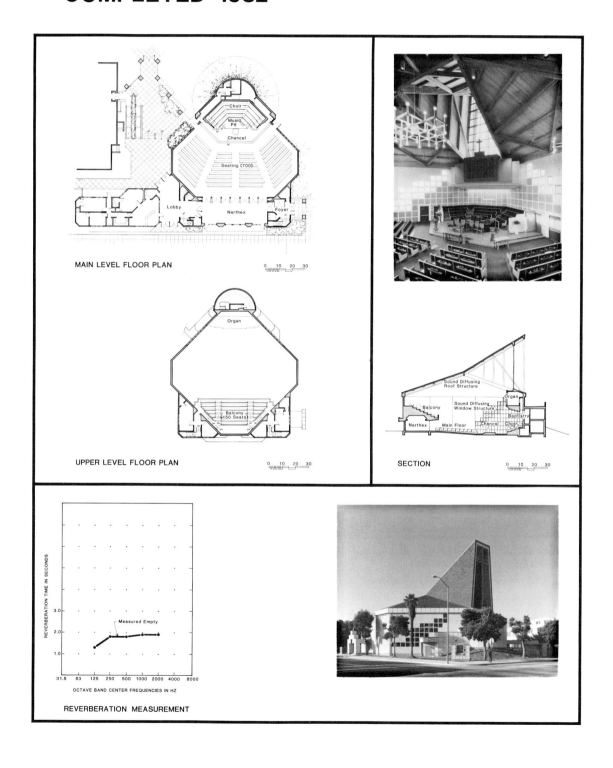

MAIN LEVEL FLOOR PLAN

Choir
Music Pit
Chancel
Seating (700)
Lobby
Narthex
Foyer

UPPER LEVEL FLOOR PLAN

Organ
Balcony (150 Seats)

SECTION

Sound Diffusing Roof Structure
Sound Diffusing Window Structure
Organ
Balcony
Baptistry
Narthex
Main Floor
Chancel
Choir

REVERBERATION MEASUREMENT

REVERBERATION TIME IN SECONDS
Measured Empty
OCTAVE BAND CENTER FREQUENCIES IN HZ

SAINT MATTHEW'S EPISCOPAL CHURCH
PACIFIC PALISADES, CALIFORNIA

COMPLETED: 1983

OWNER: Parish of St. Matthew

ARCHITECT: Moore, Ruble, Yudell
Los Angeles, California

ACOUSTICAL CONSULTANT: Purcell & Noppe & Assoc., Inc.
Chatsworth, California
Jack B. C. Purcell,
Partner in charge

COST: $2,000,000

The devastating Southern California fire of 1979 destroyed, among many other structures, the Church of St. Matthew's Parish. The determination to construct a new sanctuary on the existing site was established after a detailed study of nine sites located within the property environs. The firm of Moore, Ruble, Yudell was engaged as architects for the new structure. From the outset, a very strong emphasis was placed on providing an excellent acoustical environment for the liturgical music. The sanctuary will eventually house a Charles Fisk organ, which will be elevated on the rear wall of the sanctuary, and in turn flanked by the choir.

In order to achieve adequate reverberation time, extreme measures were taken to ensure that the wood and glass surfaces which constitute much of the interior finished structure did not function as efficient acoustical absorbers. All wood-work is backed-up with 2" of concrete, and all glass is limited to a minimum 3/8" thickness. The church is uncarpeted, with the only concession to absorption being upholstered pew cushions of 2" thickness.

Speech intelligibility relies heavily upon the installation of a highly directional sound reinforcement system, which has been designed but not installed...due to aesthetic complications.

The musical acoustics of the service are extraordinary. However, the speech will continue to suffer somewhat until the congregation accepts the sound reinforcement system design which consists of a central cluster suspended high over the altar at the apse.

PARISH OF ST. MATTHEW
PACIFIC PALISADES, CALIFORNIA
1983

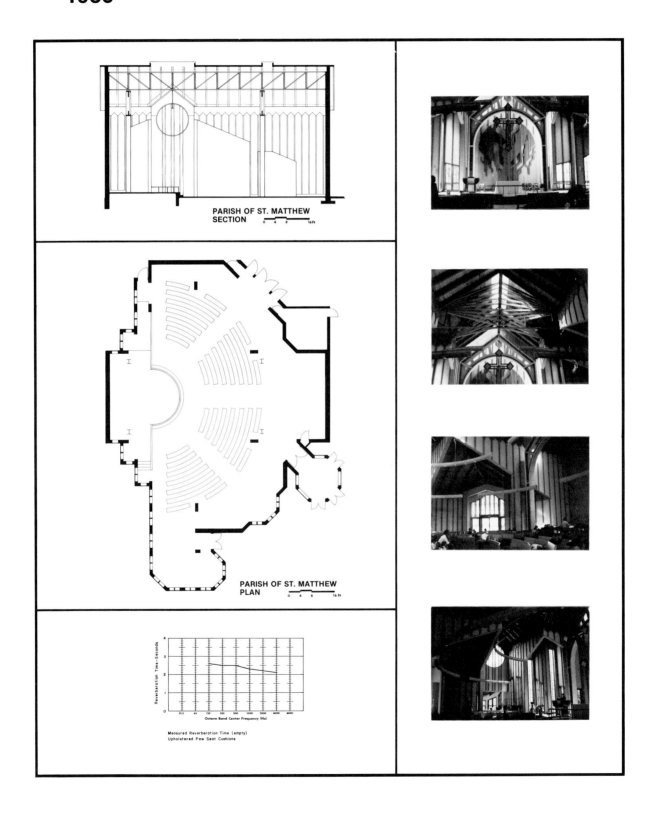

PARISH OF ST. MATTHEW
SECTION   0 4 8   16ft

PARISH OF ST. MATTHEW
PLAN   0 4 8   16 ft

Measured Reverberation Time (empty)
Upholstered Pew Seat Cushions

FIRST CHURCH OF THE NAZARENE
PASADENA, CALIFORNIA

COMPLETED: August 1980

ARCHITECT: Gaede, Alcorn & Associates
                                    Pasadena, California
                                    Carl Gaede, Project Designer

ACOUSTICAL CONSULTANT: Bolt Beranek and Newman Inc.
                                    Canoga Park, California
                                    Ronald L. McKay,
                                        Project Consultant

CONSTRUCTION COST: $7,000,000

The auditorium's circular seating plan was developed to maximize intimacy between 2500 worshipers and the platform. Above this plan the architect chose to make a powerful vertical expression with exposed wood trusses supporting a wood roof deck of eight facets and surmounted by a great lantern with stained glass windows some 90 feet above the floor. The resulting auditorium volume is 880,000 cubic feet.

Directions by the owner to the acoustical consultant were to create a "living room" environment for speech and a pleasant listening environment for music.

Extreme unevenness due to the focusing power of the auditorium's lower walls was avoided by providing hard, diffusing surfaces behind the choir and highly-absorptive surfaces around the congregation at upper and lower levels. A large sound-reflecting canopy was suspended over the platform to provide vital short-time-delay reflections to musicians on the platform and congregation members on the main floor. The canopy also houses theatrical lighting and three loudspeaker clusters. No acceptable design compromise was found to avoid the acoustical "shadowing" caused by the deep balcony overhangs above the rear main floor.

The results achieved meet the owner's directions fully. The pastor, equipped with a wireless microphone, usually roams an area of about 30-foot radius around the pulpit during his sermon. Almost every one of his words is intelligible in all 2500 seats, while listening in a relaxed manner. Music listening is pleasant, if not dramatic. Reviewing a performance by the Pasadena Chamber Orchestra, the *Los Angeles Times* commented: "The ... church sanctuary ... proved a congenial venue for music; a handsome room (that) can boast acoustics of medium-dry and clear character." The acoustical consultant considers this a fair statement.

FIRST CHURCH OF THE NAZARENE
PASADENA, CALIFORNIA
COMPLETED IN 1980

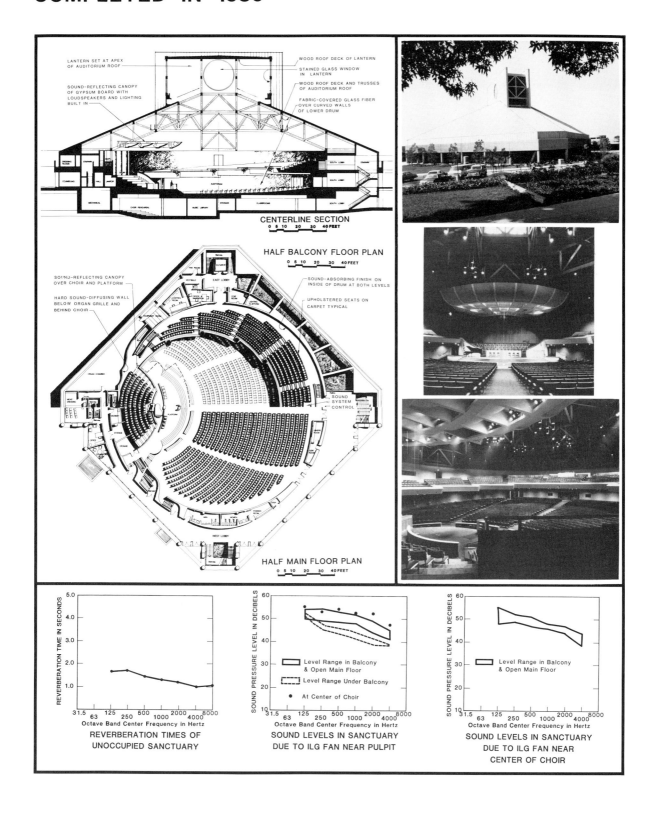

LANTERN SET AT APEX OF AUDITORIUM ROOF

SOUND-REFLECTING CANOPY OF GYPSUM BOARD WITH LOUDSPEAKERS AND LIGHTING BUILT IN

WOOD ROOF DECK OF LANTERN

STAINED GLASS WINDOW IN LANTERN

WOOD ROOF DECK AND TRUSSES OF AUDITORIUM ROOF

FABRIC-COVERED GLASS FIBER OVER CURVED WALLS OF LOWER DRUM

CENTERLINE SECTION
0 5 10 20 30 40 FEET

HALF BALCONY FLOOR PLAN
0 5 10 20 30 40 FEET

SOUND-REFLECTING CANOPY OVER CHOIR AND PLATFORM

HARD SOUND-DIFFUSING WALL BELOW ORGAN GRILLE AND BEHIND CHOIR

SOUND-ABSORBING FINISH ON INSIDE OF DRUM AT BOTH LEVELS

UPHOLSTERED SEATS ON CARPET TYPICAL

SOUND SYSTEM CONTROL

HALF MAIN FLOOR PLAN
0 5 10 20 30 40 FEET

REVERBERATION TIMES OF UNOCCUPIED SANCTUARY

REVERBERATION TIME IN SECONDS

Octave Band Center Frequency in Hertz

SOUND LEVELS IN SANCTUARY DUE TO ILG FAN NEAR PULPIT

SOUND PRESSURE LEVEL IN DECIBELS

Octave Band Center Frequency in Hertz

Level Range in Balcony & Open Main Floor
Level Range Under Balcony
At Center of Choir

SOUND LEVELS IN SANCTUARY DUE TO ILG FAN NEAR CENTER OF CHOIR

SOUND PRESSURE LEVEL IN DECIBELS

Octave Band Center Frequency in Hertz

Level Range in Balcony & Open Main Floor

TIFERETH ISRAEL SYNAGOGUE
SAN DIEGO, CALIFORNIA

COMPLETED:	1978
OWNER:	Congregation Tifereth Israel
ARCHITECT:	Macy, Henderson and Cole San Diego, California Alfonso Macy, Project Architect
ENGINEERS:	George R. Saunders & Associates (structural) Dunn, Lee, Smith & Klein (mechanical/electrical)
LANDSCAPE ARCHITECT:	Kawasaki, Theilacker & Associates

Tifereth Israel is a Conservative congregation at present serving 670 families.

The hilltop sanctuary is well isolated from exterior noise; it has 384 permanent seats, with capacity for up to 200 temporary seats, a 30-voice adult choir and a 65-voice childrens' choir. For High Holy Day assemblies, the movable partitions separating the sanctuary from the social hall are opened to accommodate a congregation of approximately 2000.

The sanctuary walls and ceiling are predominantly sound-reflective. The carpeted floor and cushioned pews provide control of reverberation. The choir is accompanied by a piano or small electronic organ.

For speech and music reinforcement, directional loudspeakers mounted on either side of the Ark provide good coverage for sanctuary seating. Listening positions for the hearing-impaired are provided in ten locations scattered throughout the sanctuary. In the full assembly condition, the overflow seating is served by a ceiling-mounted, time-delayed system. The latter system also provides sound reinforcement from the stage when the social hall is used independently.

TIFERETH ISRAEL SYNAGOGUE
SAN DIEGO, CALIFORNIA
1978

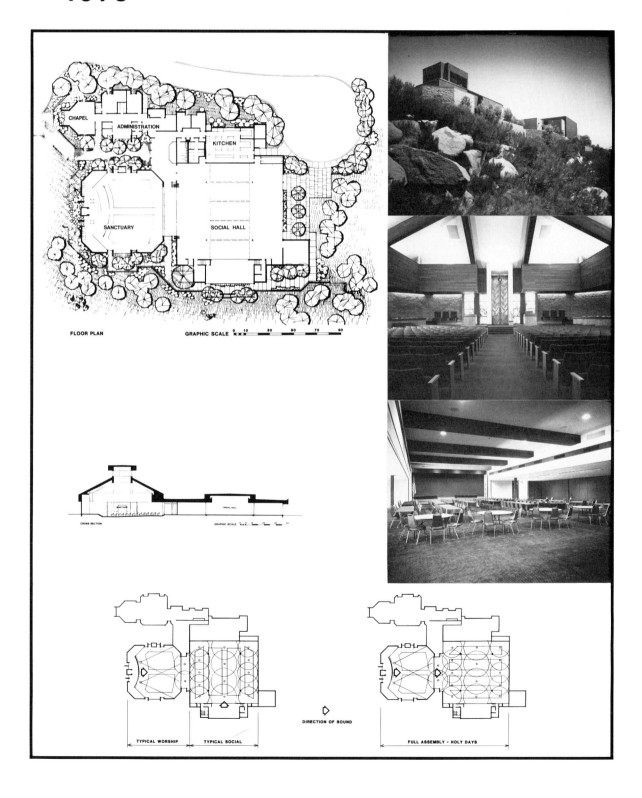

MISSION VALLEY FREE METHODIST CHURCH
SAN GABRIEL, CALIFORNIA

COMPLETED: 1984

OWNER: Mission Valley Free Methodist
                                            Church

ARCHITECT: Roy Takei

ACOUSTICAL CONSULTANT: Dr. Marshall Long
                                        Marshall Long/Acoustics
                                        Santa Monica, California

COST: $550,000, including organ and
                                            sound system

Mission Valley Free Methodist Church, which is currently under construction, serves an active Korean-American congregation in the San Gabriel Valley area of Los Angeles, California. The object of the acoustical design was to obtain a suitably reverberant environment for choral and organ music while using a directional sound system to provide the necessary intelligibility for speech. The first goal was accomplished with due consideration for the client's desire to have carpet on the floor and to use a single layer of 5/8" gypsum board on the walls due to budgetary constraints. The square floor plan necessitated the use of absorbent wall panels to reduce potential slap. The result was a mid-frequency reverberation time of about 1.5 seconds which rises nicely at 250 Hz and then drops at 125 Hz due to the absorption of the gypsum board. This yields a space which is reasonably live for religious music in all but the lowest frequency bands.

The sound system design was done using the computer analysis technique which had been developed earlier. The design goal was to minimize the direct field seat-to-seat variation in sound pressure level by careful selection of the system components, their locations and aim points. The maximum predicted variation was plus or minus 2.2 dB from 125 to 500 Hz and plus or minus 1.5 dB from 1000 to 4 kHz in the direct sound field. A distributed overhead system was also provided for the narthex, vestry, choir and for the sound booth. Selected pews are equipped with special head sets for the hearing-impaired.

The church is a fine example of what can be done aesthetically in a small floor plan while giving ample consideration to acoustical concerns.

MISSION VALLEY FREE METHODIST CHURCH
SAN GABRIEL, CALIFORNIA
UNDER CONSTRUCTION

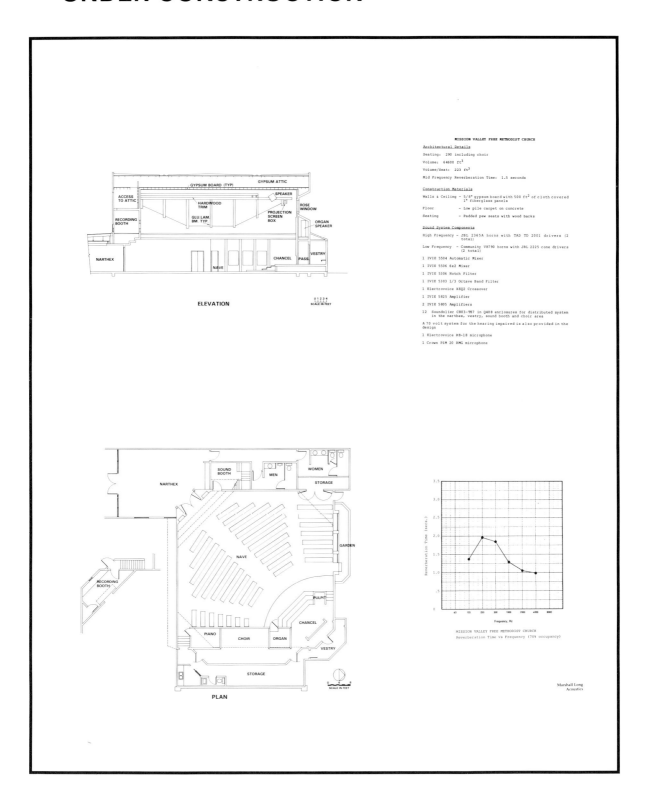

ELEVATION

MISSION VALLEY FREE METHODIST CHURCH

Architectural Details

Seating: 290 including choir

Volume: 64600 ft^3

Volume/Seat: 223 ft^3

Mid Frequency Reverberation Time: 1.5 seconds

Construction Materials

Walls & Ceiling - 5/8" gypsum board with 500 ft^2 of cloth covered 1" fiberglass panels

Floor   - Low pile carpet on concrete

Seating   - Padded pew seats with wood backs

Sound System Components

High Frequency - JBL 2365A horns with TAD TD 2001 drivers (2 total)

Low Frequency - Community VB790 horns with JBL 2225 cone drivers (2 total)

1 IVIE 5504 Automatic Mixer

1 IVIE 5506 6x2 Mixer

1 IVIE 5306 Notch Filter

1 IVIE 5303 1/3 Octave Band Filter

1 Electrovoice XEQ2 Crossover

1 IVIE 5825 Amplifier

2 IVIE 5805 Amplifiers

12 Soundolier C803-T87 in Q408 enclosures for distributed system in the narthex, vestry, sound booth and choir area

A 70 volt system for the hearing impaired is also provided in the design

1 Electrovoice RE-18 microphone

1 Crown PZM 20 RMG microphone

MISSION VALLEY FREE METHODIST CHURCH
Reverberation Time vs Frequency (70% occupancy)

PLAN

Marshall Long
Acoustics

MEMORIAL CHURCH
STANFORD UNIVERSITY
STANFORD, CALIFORNIA

RENOVATION COMPLETED: 1982

OWNER: Stanford University

ARCHITECT FOR   Esherick, Homsey, Dodge & Davis
RENOVATION: San Francisco, California

ACOUSTICAL CONSULTANT   Bolt Beranek and Newman Inc.
FOR RENOVATION: Canoga Park, California

Memorial Church was the focal point of the original Stanford University campus plan conceived by Leland Stanford. On its completion around 1904 it was dedicated in his honor by his widow.

In April 1906 the church was severely damaged during the great earthquake. The main tower over the crossing collapsed and was never rebuilt, but the remainder of the building was restored. In recent years, the entire structure has been strengthened to meet existing seismic design requirements. However, the transept balconies are not used now because the exit stairs do not meet fire safety standards.

Around 1910 the wood plank ceiling of the sanctuary was covered with 3″ thick hair felt, evidently to reduce reverberation sufficiently to make speech reasonably intelligible. While this was only partially successful, it adversely affected the acoustical performance of the 1901 Murray Harris organ, and various attempts were made to offset this by enlarging the organ and raising wind pressures.

In conjunction with the installation in 1984 of a tracker-action organ built by Charles Fisk, the hair felt was removed from all areas except the transepts. The resulting increase in reverberance is particularly gratifying for organ and choral works. The new organ is in the balcony between the two sections of the still-used Murray Harris.

To accommodate the increased reverberance a new speech reinforcement system has been installed. This incorporates highly-directional horn loudspeakers, located so as to minimize their visual obtrusiveness and time-delayed to retain the precedence effect from the person speaking. Wireless microphones are being used successfully during services which require speech from many locations in the chancel.

MEMORIAL CHURCH, STANFORD UNIVERSITY
STANFORD, CALIFORNIA
RENOVATION COMPLETED 1982

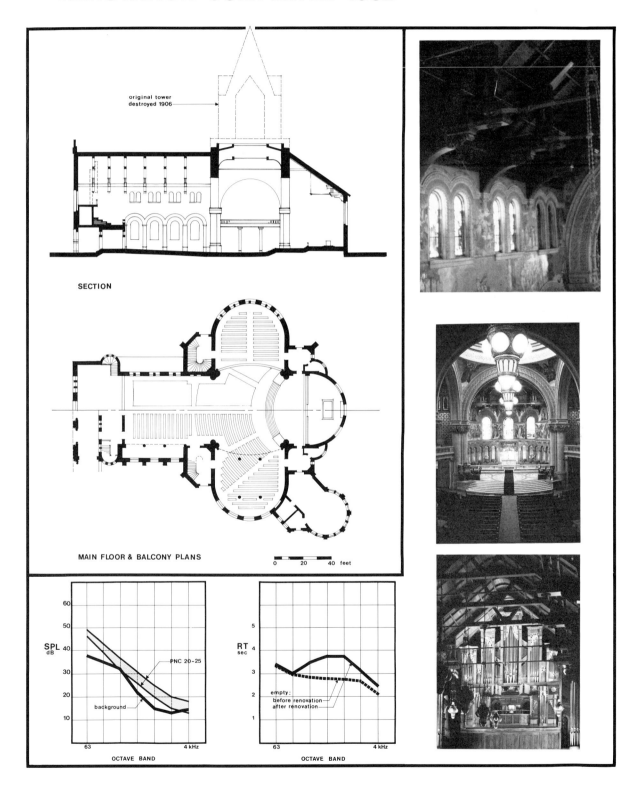

original tower
destroyed 1906

SECTION

MAIN FLOOR & BALCONY PLANS

0   20   40 feet

SPL
dB

PNC 20-25

background

OCTAVE BAND

63   4 kHz

RT
sec

empty:
before renovation
after renovation

OCTAVE BAND

63   4 kHz

CROSSROADS CHURCH OF CHRIST
GAINESVILLE, FLORIDA

COMPLETED:	1972
OWNER:	Crossroads Church of Christ
ARCHITECT:	James McGinley, AIA, Architect
ACOUSTICAL CONSULTANT:	Bertram Y. Kinzey, Jr. Gainesville, Florida
STRUCTURAL ENGINEER:	Manuel Solis
MECHANICAL ENGINEER:	Spence & Associates
CONSTRUCTION COST:	$480,000

Unaccompanied congregational singing required excellent acoustical support from the architectural design. Consequently, all surfaces were made sound reflective except for a narrow band of acoustical tile above the cove lighting on the rear wall. Zig-zag rear wall surfaces were used to avoid sound focussing to the front. Ceiling panels were hung at strategic points to direct sound to the congregation rather than have the ceiling return an echo to the pulpit. No electronic speech reinforcement was installed.

The drawings show the church as originally built. The auditorium was later enlarged by removing the zig-zag walls. Electronic speech reinforcement was added by installing two horns in the high apex of the ceiling. The building has also been enlarged at its eastern end. The photographs and acoustical measurements are for the building in its expanded configuration.

CROSSROADS CHURCH OF CHRIST
GAINESVILLE, FLORIDA
1972

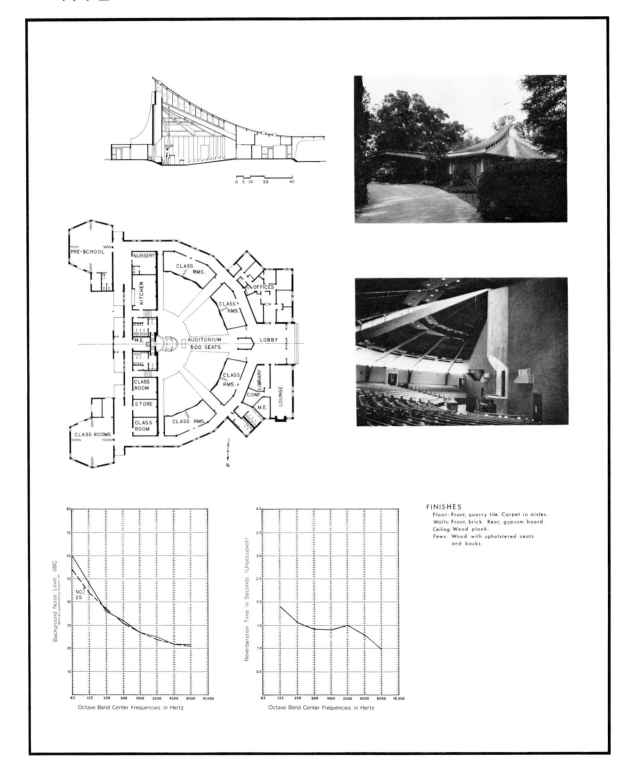

FINISHES
Floor: Front, quarry tile. Carpet in aisles.
Walls: Front, brick.. Rear, gypsum board.
Ceiling: Wood plank.
Pews: Wood with upholstered seats
and backs.

FIRST LUTHERAN CHURCH
GAINESVILLE, FLORIDA

COMPLETED:	1966
OWNER:	First Lutheran Church
ARCHITECT:	William C. Grobe, AIA,
ACOUSTICAL CONSULTANT:	Bertram Y. Kinzey, Jr. Gainesville, Florida
STRUCTURAL CONSULTANT:	M. H. Johnson
MECHANICAL & ELECTRICAL ENGINEER:	Ebaugh & Goethe, Inc.
ORGAN BUILDER:	Kinzey-Angerstein Organ Co.
CONSTRUCTION COST:	$200,000

The church design was predicated on good hearing of both speech and music without any electronic reinforcement.

The chancel surfaces of brick, vinyl tile and wood project the voice to the congregation adequately even when the celebrant faces the altar. The upper portion of the chancel ceiling has panels of furred acoustical tile to prevent an echo back to the speaking position. Tilted glass and absorbent surfaces at the narthex wall eliminate echoes to the chancel.

The choir gallery has zig-zag side walls and all hard surfaces for maximum diffusion and projection of music. The space was designed in anticipation of the later installation of the organ which occurred in 1982.

FIRST LUTHERAN CHURCH
GAINESVILLE, FLORIDA
1966

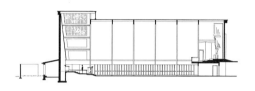

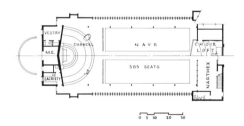

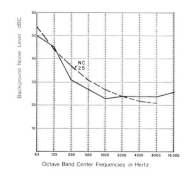

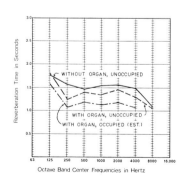

FINISHES

Floor: Vinyl asbestos tile on concrete.
    Carpeted center aisle.
Walls: Chancel, brick. Choir loft, gypsum board.
    Rear nave, fiberglass absorbent and
    tilted glass.
Ceiling: Wood plank.
Pews: Wood with seat cushions.

FIRST BAPTIST CHURCH
ORLANDO, FLORIDA

UNDER CONSTRUCTION:	1985 Planned Completion Date
ARCHITECT:	Hatfield Halcomb Architects Dallas, Texas
ACOUSTICAL CONSULTANT:	Joiner-Pelton-Rose, Inc. Dallas, Texas

This represents a design increasingly popular with large Baptist congregations—a fan-shaped room whose large balcony terminates in side arms that sweep down to the floor.

Upper rear walls are absorptive to minimize sound system echo;, walls and the highly modeled ceiling are gypsum board; floors are carpeted: and pews are upholstered. Volume ratio is approximately 400 cubic feet per seat, based on a capacity of 5000.

The central cluster sound system can "see" the under-balcony seating. A 32-input console is planned, with separate video, broadcast, and house mixes. 275 microphone inputs are located in the sanctuary. Provisions for future expansion includes stereo cluster additions for music reinforcement.

Extensive rehearsal and other support facilities are housed in the same building as the sanctuary. HVAC noise and vibration isolation measures are also part of the integrated acoustical design package.

FIRST BAPTIST CHURCH
ORLANDO, FLORIDA
COMPLETION SCHEDULED 1985

JOINER-PELTON-ROSE, INC

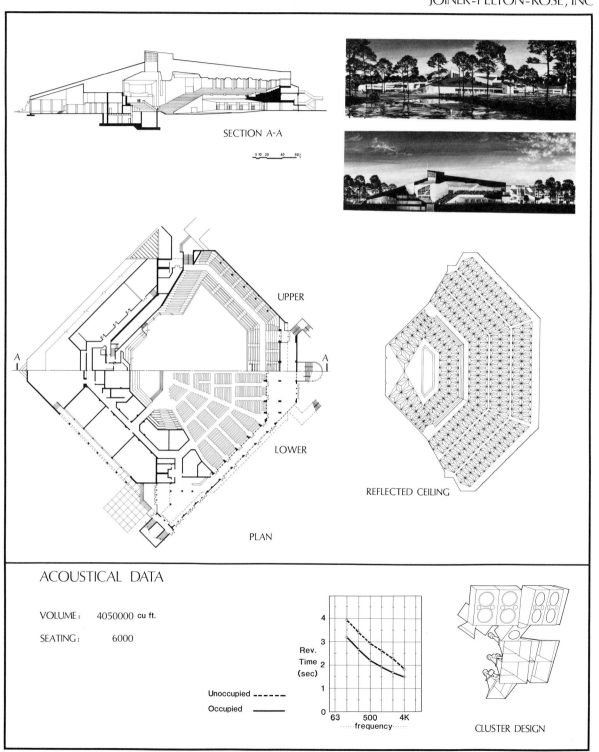

SECTION A-A

5 10 20   40   60 0

UPPER

A   A

LOWER

PLAN

REFLECTED CEILING

ACOUSTICAL DATA

VOLUME: 4050000 cu ft.

SEATING: 6000

Rev.
Time
(sec)

4
3
2
1
0

63   500   4K

frequency

Unoccupied ------
Occupied ——

CLUSTER DESIGN

SAINT MARGARET MARY CATHOLIC CHURCH
WINTER PARK, FLORIDA

COMPLETED: 1983

ARCHITECT: Rick Swisher

ACOUSTICAL CONSULTANT: Dr. Marshall Long
                                        Marshall Long/Acoustics

COST: $25,000 for the sound system
                                        and design

The semicircular construction of Saint Margaret Mary Church presented a number of acoustical challenges. First was severe focusing from the rear wall to the front rows and the sanctuary, compounded by distributed column speakers around the perimeter of the seating area including the rear wall. The result was a very long delay particularly in the front rows which made intelligibility extremely poor. For aesthetic reasons the church was strongly opposed to a central cluster system, which would also have had the problem of being close to the center of curvature of the rear walls. Thus the sound system design placed the speakers in the two large vertical columns on either side of the sanctuary. The columns were modified by increasing the size of the grille-cloth covered opening (see pre-construction photo).

To resolve the problems of coverage and feedback a computer program was written to predict the sound level at any point for any speaker location, aim point and rotation angle. This program allowed virtually seamless coverage to be predicted using unusual speaker locations. It also allowed crossfire coverage of each rear half of the church from the opposite column. This corrected a hole which would otherwise have occurred in the front center of the nave.

Another problem was the location of the organ speakers in the column where the new sound system was to go. This location created difficulty in coordinating choir, organist and soloist due to the difference in delay times between the speakers and the choir. The solution was to build risers for the choir and a music storage room, and to relocate the organ speakers on the ceiling of this room. This placed the organ speakers close to the choir and gave the choir useful reflecting surfaces at its back. It also allowed the organist to hear the organ speakers much better than in the previous configuration. The result was quite successful.

Intelligibility from the directional high frequency and low frequency horns is excellent in all parts of the church. Reflections from the back wall have been virtually eliminated and partial removal of the rear wall absorption is contemplated.

SAINT MARGARET MARY CATHOLIC CHURCH
WINTER PARK, FLORIDA
1983

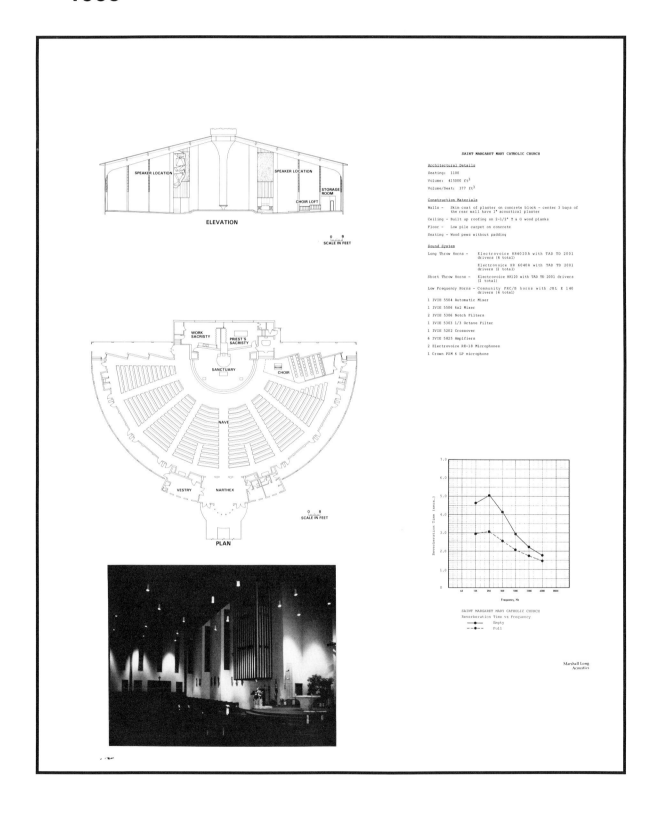

ELEVATION

0   8
SCALE IN FEET

SPEAKER LOCATION

SPEAKER LOCATION

STORAGE ROOM

CHOIR LOFT

WORK SACRISTY

PRIEST'S SACRISTY

SANCTUARY

CHOIR

NAVE

VESTRY   NARTHEX

0   8
SCALE IN FEET

PLAN

SAINT MARGARET MARY CATHOLIC CHURCH

Architectural Details

Seating: 1100

Volume: 415000 ft^3

Volume/Seat: 377 ft^3

Construction Materials

Walls –   Skim coat of plaster on concrete block – center 3 bays of
          the rear wall have 1" acoustical plaster

Ceiling – Built up roofing on 2-1/2" T & G wood planks

Floor –   Low pile carpet on concrete

Seating – Wood pews without padding

Sound System

Long Throw Horns –   Electrovoice HR4020A with TAD TD 2001
                       drivers (4 total)

                       Electrovoice HR 6040A with TAD TD 2001
                       drivers (2 total)

Short Throw Horns –   Electrovoice HR120 with TAD TD 2001 drivers
                       (2 total)

Low Frequency Horns – Community FRC/B horns with JBL E 140
                      drivers (4 total)

1 IVIE 5504 Automatic Mixer

1 IVIE 5506 6x2 Mixer

2 IVIE 5306 Notch Filters

1 IVIE 5303 1/3 Octave Filter

1 IVIE 5202 Crossover

6 IVIE 5825 Amplifiers

2 Electrovoice RE-18 Microphones

1 Crown P2M 6 LP microphone

SAINT MARGARET MARY CATHOLIC CHURCH
Reverberation Time vs Frequency
———●——— Empty
– –●– – Full

Marshall Long
Acoustics

FIRST BAPTIST CHURCH
KENNER, LOUISIANA

COMPLETED: 1983

ARCHITECT: Ellerbe Architects Engineers
                                         Planners
                                    New Orleans, Louisiana

ACOUSTICAL CONSULTANT: Joiner-Pelton-Rose, Inc.
                                    Dallas, Texas

The sanctuary is a 90-degree, fan-shaped auditorium seating 2,000. Upper rear walls are splayed to promote diffusion and improve reverberance. Sightlines to the raised platform and raised choir are excellent. The nose of the balcony is shaped to prevent focusing. The audio control position is centered at the front of the balcony.

Finishes include gypsum board ceiling and walls, carpeted floors, and pews with cushioned seats and hard backs. Volume ratio is 193 cubic feet per seat. The choir rehearsal space is located directly behind the sanctuary choir area.

The sound system is the central-cluster type with time-delayed under-balcony speakers. Additional speakers are located in the circulation corridor behind the sanctuary.

The church is located one-half mile from Runway 10/28 of New Orleans International Airport. As it is subject to overflights producing levels in excess of 90 dBA, building skin construction was modified to achieve a satisfactory noise level inside the sanctuary.

FIRST BAPTIST CHURCH
KENNER, LOUISIANA
COMPLETED 1983

JOINER-PELTON-ROSE, INC

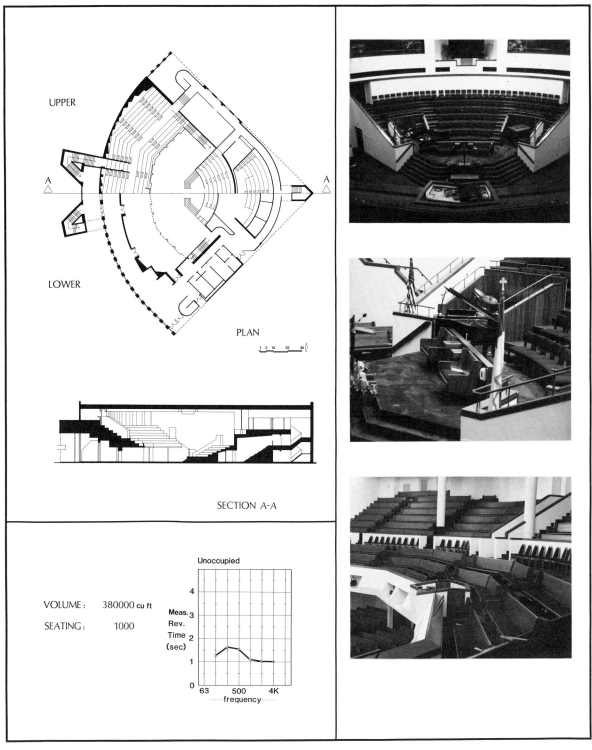

UPPER

LOWER

A

A

PLAN

1 5 10   20   30

SECTION A-A

VOLUME: 380000 cu ft

SEATING: 1000

Unoccupied

Meas.
Rev.
Time
(sec)

4

3

2

1

0

63   500   4K

········ frequency ········

RANDALL MEMORIAL BAPTIST CHURCH
AMHERST, NEW YORK

COMPLETED: 1969

ARCHITECT: Shelgren, Patterson & Marzec
                                    Buffalo, New York

ACOUSTICAL CONSULTANT: Angevine Acoustical
                                        Consultants, Inc.
                                    West Falls, New York

The Randall Memorial Baptist Church was built as an addition to the church's existing school building and as a replacement for a smaller sanctuary. The church is located under the final air approach to the instrument-landing runway of the Greater Buffalo International Airport, which handles 80% of traffic landing and 15% of traffic taking off. Heavy aircraft are at an altitude of 1500 feet and light aircraft at only 800 feet.

Due to these extraordinary conditions, special considerations had to be taken to insulate church services from air traffic noise. These included a reinforced roof ventilated in the eaves and inoperable double-glazed windows. The mechanical room for the HVAC equipment also needed to be isolated from the nave above with a plaster ceiling and isolation mounts on the equipment.

The church is equipped with a grand piano, a projection and radio broadcast booth, video cameras, and an impressive Moller pipe organ, including a separate blower room with 2″ cork insulation and baffled air intake.

RANDALL MEMORIAL BAPTIST CHURCH
AMHERST, NEW YORK
COMPLETED — 1969

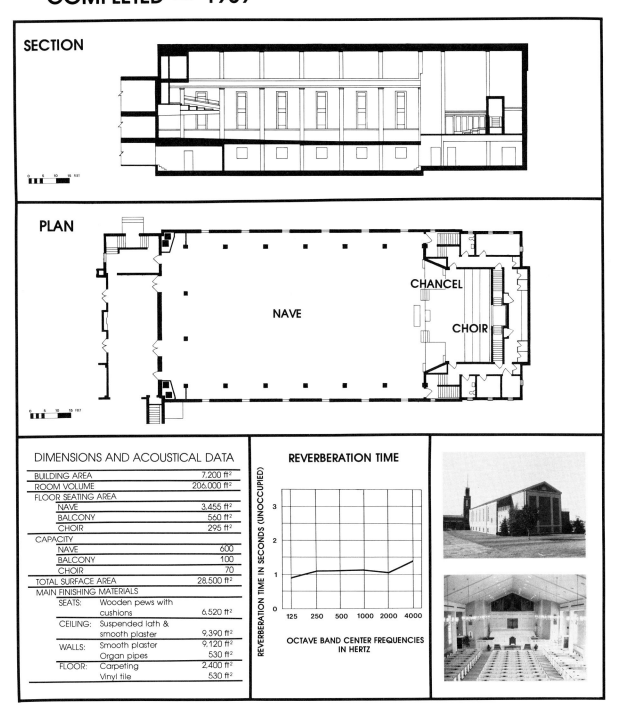

SECTION

0 5 10 15 FEET

PLAN

NAVE

CHANCEL

CHOIR

0 5 10 15 FEET

DIMENSIONS AND ACOUSTICAL DATA

BUILDING AREA		7,200 ft²
ROOM VOLUME		206,000 ft²
FLOOR SEATING AREA		
	NAVE	3,455 ft²
	BALCONY	560 ft²
	CHOIR	295 ft²
CAPACITY		
	NAVE	600
	BALCONY	100
	CHOIR	70
TOTAL SURFACE AREA		28,500 ft²
MAIN FINISHING MATERIALS		
SEATS:	Wooden pews with cushions	6,520 ft²
CEILING:	Suspended lath & smooth plaster	9,390 ft²
WALLS:	Smooth plaster	9,120 ft²
	Organ pipes	530 ft²
FLOOR:	Carpeting	2,400 ft²
	Vinyl tile	530 ft²

REVERBERATION TIME

REVERBERATION TIME IN SECONDS (UNOCCUPIED)

3

2

1

0

125   250   500   1000   2000   4000

OCTAVE BAND CENTER FREQUENCIES
IN HERTZ

LAKE AVENUE MEMORIAL BAPTIST CHURCH
ROCHESTER, NEW YORK

COMPLETED: 1975

ARCHITECT: Parks, Morin, Hall & Brennan
                                    Rochester, New York

ACOUSTICAL CONSULTANT: Angevine Acoustical
                                        Consultants, Inc.
                                    West Falls, New York

The present Lake Avenue Memorial Baptist Church is actually the third house of worship to be built on the same site. The first was a small missionary chapel, the second a larger structure that subsequently grew through renovations as adjoining properties were acquired. A fire destroyed the structure in 1972, and soon after the plans for the new building were completed.

It was desired to build a functional and multi-purpose building at lowest possible cost on the original site, which is a triangular lot. Besides the main sanctuary, it was planned to include a social gathering hall with adjoining kitchen area, a day-care center, a music and choir robing room, classroom space, and offices.

The nave is roughly in the shape of a right triangle, with ceiling sloping up towards the chancel. The Holtkamp organ is located to the left, with pipes recessed in an alcove. Five separate sound systems were designed for the building. The reinforcement speakers for the nave are housed in overhead cylindrical fixtures similar in shape to the lights. The windows are deeply recessed and angular, reinforcing the vertical dimensions and the unique shape of the structure.

LAKE AVENUE MEMORIAL BAPTIST CHURCH
ROCHESTER, NEW YORK
COMPLETED — 1975

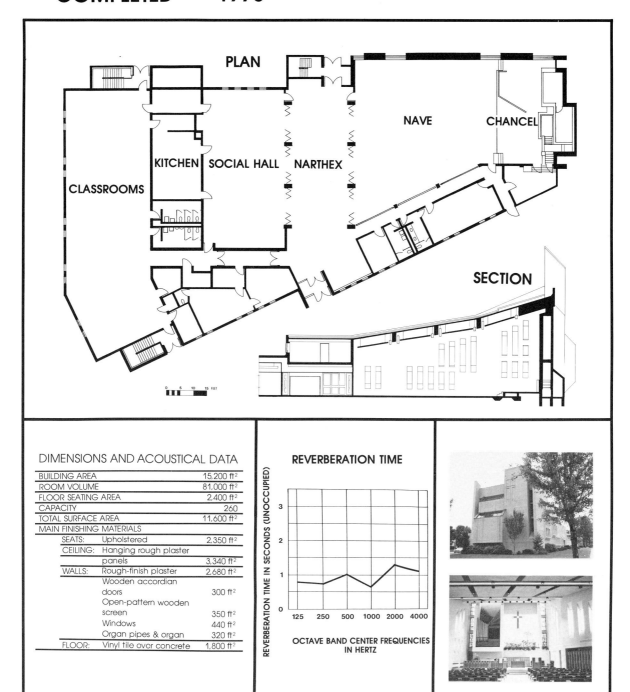

PLAN

CLASSROOMS   KITCHEN   SOCIAL HALL   NARTHEX   NAVE   CHANCEL

SECTION

0   5   10   15 FEET

DIMENSIONS AND ACOUSTICAL DATA

BUILDING AREA		15,200 ft²
ROOM VOLUME		81,000 ft²
FLOOR SEATING AREA		2,400 ft²
CAPACITY		260
TOTAL SURFACE AREA		11,600 ft²
MAIN FINISHING MATERIALS		
SEATS:	Upholstered	2,350 ft²
CEILING:	Hanging rough plaster panels	3,340 ft²
WALLS:	Rough-finish plaster	2,680 ft²
	Wooden accordian doors	300 ft²
	Open-pattern wooden screen	350 ft²
	Windows	440 ft²
	Organ pipes & organ	320 ft²
FLOOR:	Vinyl tile over concrete	1,800 ft²

REVERBERATION TIME

REVERBERATION TIME IN SECONDS (UNOCCUPIED)

125   250   500   1000   2000   4000

OCTAVE BAND CENTER FREQUENCIES
IN HERTZ

INTERFAITH CHAPEL
UNIVERSITY OF ROCHESTER
ROCHESTER, NEW YORK

COMPLETED: 1975

ARCHITECT: Wiard and Burwell

ACOUSTICAL CONSULTANT: Angevine Acoustical
                                        Consultants, Inc.
                                    West Falls, New York

ACOUSTICAL MODELING: Auguste C. Raes
                                    Brussels, Belgium

The University of Rochester's Interfaith Chapel is a nondenominational space of worship constructed on three levels, beginning at the elevation of the Genesee River and ascending to campus level. The chapel serves two purposes, first to provide a center for the university's comprehensive religious program which includes worship, counseling, teaching and service activities: and, second, to provide a structural symbol of the university's belief in the importance of religious expression on campus.

Four concrete arches rise from a concrete and brick base into a tower of four large stained glass windows which gather light into the main sanctuary on the campus level. Below on the middle level are the Fellowship Room, Chaplain's office, library, and choir robing and conference room. On the lowest level, the River Chapel seats 320 people for small services and weddings, with three wings or meditation chapels seating up to 40 people each for Jewish, Roman Catholic, and Protestant services. The organ in the main sanctuary was provided by Casavant Freres, Ltd. of Ste. Hyacinthe, Quebec.

UNIVERSITY OF ROCHESTER
INTERFAITH CHAPEL
ROCHESTER, NEW YORK
COMPLETED — 1975

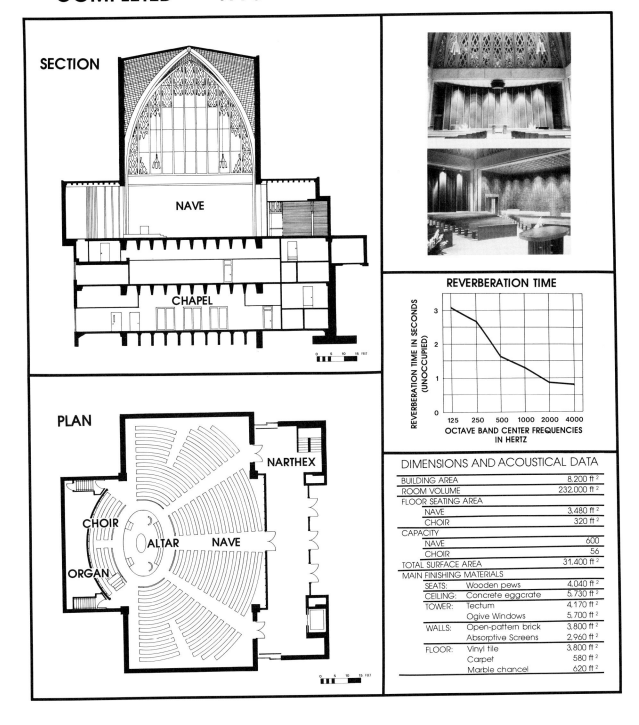

SECTION

NAVE

CHAPEL

0 5 10 15 FEET

PLAN

NARTHEX

CHOIR

ORGAN

ALTAR   NAVE

0 5 10 15 FEET

REVERBERATION TIME

REVERBERATION TIME IN SECONDS (UNOCCUPIED)

125 250 500 1000 2000 4000

OCTAVE BAND CENTER FREQUENCIES IN HERTZ

DIMENSIONS AND ACOUSTICAL DATA

BUILDING AREA		8,200 ft^2
ROOM VOLUME		232,000 ft^2
FLOOR SEATING AREA		
	NAVE	3,480 ft^2
	CHOIR	320 ft^2
CAPACITY		
	NAVE	600
	CHOIR	56
TOTAL SURFACE AREA		31,400 ft^2
MAIN FINISHING MATERIALS		
SEATS:	Wooden pews	4,040 ft^2
CEILING:	Concrete eggcrate	5,730 ft^2
TOWER:	Tectum	4,170 ft^2
	Ogive Windows	5,700 ft^2
WALLS:	Open-pattern brick	3,800 ft^2
	Absorptive Screens	2,960 ft^2
FLOOR:	Vinyl tile	3,800 ft^2
	Carpet	580 ft^2
	Marble chancel	620 ft^2

DUKE UNIVERSITY CHAPEL
DURHAM, NORTH CAROLINA

RENOVATION COMPLETED: 1973

OWNER: Duke University

ACOUSTICAL CONSULTANT   Bolt Beranek and Newman Inc.
FOR RENOVATION: Cambridge, Massachusetts

Designed by Horace Trumbauer of Philadelphia and constructed from 1930 to 1932, the Duke University Chapel is a neo-Gothic design in the tradition of many of the great churches in the eastern United States.

It is 264 feet long, 54 feet wide in the nave, 30 feet wide in the chancel, and 112 feet wide across the transepts. The vaulting height at the crossing is 75 feet; the total volume of the space is approximately one million cubic feet.

The interior finish materials are limestone - chiefly in the choir and lower walls - and elsewhere Akoustolith, a porous tile similar in appearance to limestone, which was designed by W. C. Sabine and R. Guastavino for control of reverberation to enhance intelligibility in large volumes such as this.

In 1969 the University commissioned D. A. Flentrop of Holland to build a new organ. It was agreed that the reverberation time should be increased to allow the new organ to be heard to best effect.

The acoustical consultants found a coating which would seal the porous surface of the Akoustolith without changing its appearance. Laboratory tests showed that two coats of sealant were required to adequately reduce its porosity, but these results could not be emulated by painters working on 70 foot high scaffolds in temperatures of over 90°F. A further two coats were applied, and the results were deemed satisfactory by the organ builder and the users.

In conjunction with the increase in reverberation, a new speech reinforcement system was installed. The system utilizes pairs of time-delayed column loudspeakers located along the nave. While their appearance is hardly in the neo-Gothic spirit, they add a level of intelligibility heretofore unknown.

DUKE UNIVERSITY CHAPEL
DURHAM, NORTH CAROLINA
RENOVATION COMPLETED 1973

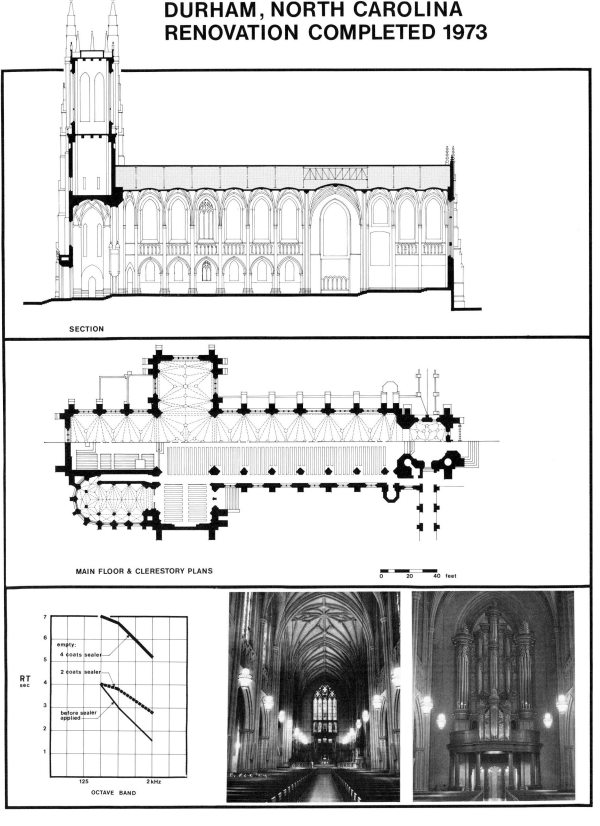

SECTION

MAIN FLOOR & CLERESTORY PLANS

0   20   40 feet

RT
sec

empty:

4 coats sealer

2 coats sealer

before sealer
applied

125   2 kHz

OCTAVE BAND

CHAPEL AT UNIVERSITY PARK
AKRON, OHIO

COMPLETED: 1972

ARCHITECT: Keith Haag Associates
                                              Cuyahoga Falls, Ohio

ACOUSTICAL CONSULTANT: Jaffe Acoustics, Inc.
                                              Norwalk, Connecticut

The complex program for the facility included seating for over 3000 people and a
podium which would support a choir of nearly 175. This yielded an extremely large
volume per person in order to maintain reasonable sight lines.

Requirements also demanded an acoustical environment which would serve to provide
excellent speech intelligibility and also provide the warmth necessary for choral presentations.

The resulting design employed absorption sufficient to establish a reverberation time of
1.4 seconds. An electronic reverberant field energizer was installed to lengthen the reverberation time to 2.1 seconds for musical programs. The system was designed with an
on/off switch so that it could be controlled during any given program.

CHAPEL AT UNIVERSITY PARK

AKRON , OHIO

CONSTRUCTION COMPLETED — 1972

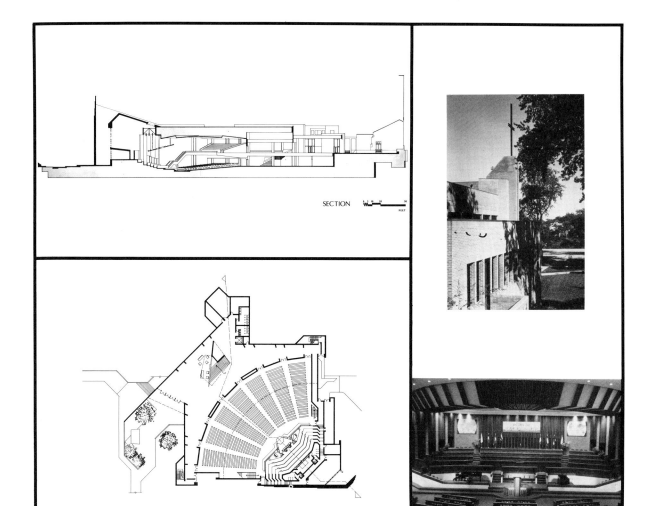

SECTION

PLAN

ACOUSTIC   DATA

VOLUME OF HALL — V : **502,000** ft^3

REVERBERATION TIME : **1.4** sec.

SEATS IN AUDIENCE — N_A : **3000** seats

INITIAL TIME DELAY GAP : **16** msec.

AUDIENCE SEATING AREA — S_A : **18,000** ft^2

$S_T = S_A + S_P$: **21,000** ft^2

S_A / N_A : **6.0** ft^2 / pers.

PODIUM AREA — S_P : **3000** ft^2

V/S_T : **42**

ST. JAMES' CHURCH OF WHITE OAK
CINCINNATI, OHIO

COMPLETED:	1981
OWNER:	Archdiocese of Cincinnati
ARCHITECT:	McClorey & Savage
ACOUSTICAL CONSULTANT:	Daniel W. Martin Cincinnati, Ohio
ENGINEERS:	Clem Fox (Structural) Robert Cassady (HVAC)
TOTAL CONSTRUCTION COSTS:	$1,150,000

St. James' Church of White Oak is a worship facility for a large parish in the suburbs near Cincinnati. The worship space consists of two parts connected by a sanctuary and choir space. The smaller part, Blessed Sacrament Chapel, seats 250 people plus the choir. The main body seats 750 for a total of approximately 1040 including the choir.

During the week a retractable partition extends between the main body and the sanctuary, reducing the active space to chapel size. Consequently, three different acoustical conditions were studied: chapel plus sanctuary, main body plus sanctuary plus chapel, and main body alone. The last condition was not a primary consideration but was planned acoustically for possible future needs.

The high central ceiling over the sanctuary slopes downward gently toward the rear in both directions. Sound reinforcement loudspeakers are centrally located near ceiling level on both sides of the partition. The upper sidewalls in both spaces are splayed inward at the rear. The lower sidewalls are parallel but are shaped to provide sound diffusion.

Ceiling height is reduced (see dashed lines on the plan) over the side and rear aisles in the chapel, and over the side seating areas of the main body, where the ceiling is inclined upward to the inner edges.

The architects were fully cooperative in the acoustical planning. The engineers provided low-velocity air conditioning as recommended. Pew cushions recommended for sound stabilization were not acceptable to the church, so absorptive ceiling was added over the chapel aisles, and more carpet was provided in the sanctuary. Results have been quite satisfactory, from an acoustical standpoint, in both the principal modes of usage.

ST.JAMES' CHURCH
CINCINNATI, OHIO
COMPLETED 1981

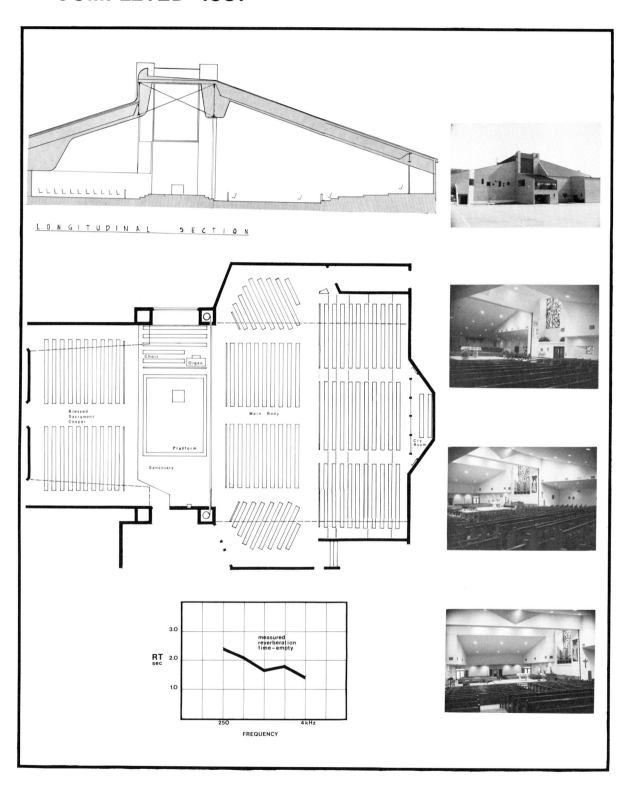

LONGITUDINAL SECTION

Choir

Organ

Blessed
Sacrament
Chapel

Main Body

Platform

Cry
Room

Sanctuary

3.0

RT
sec

2.0

1.0

measured
reverberation
time – empty

250

4 kHz

FREQUENCY

GRACE BRETHREN CHURCH
COLUMBUS, OHIO

COMPLETED:	October 1983
ARCHITECT:	James Monsul & Associates MLM Architects Consulting Architect
ACOUSTICAL CONSULTANT:	Angelo J. Campanella, ACCULAB
DESIGN/BUILD CONTRACTOR:	Service Products Buildings,Inc.
TOTAL CONSTRUCTION COST:	$2,500,000 (building only)

Columbus Grace Brethren Church is part of a 90-acre religious, K through 12 educational, sports and retirement facility. This building offers 58,000 square feet of air-conditioned space for worship and education. The sanctuary has an initial capacity of over 3,000 seats with choir of 200 for worship and for orchestra and choir productions. Other uses include pre-school day classes and practice for orchestra and choir. Future capabilities include video and T.V. production. An additional 2,000 future seats will occupy the balcony wings and replace classrooms.

The pastor's podium thrusts into the semi-circular seating area. The long steel roof spans require few interior columns. All pews are upholstered, with bare concrete floor and carpeted aisles. Ceiling and sidewall absorption limit the reverberation time of this 850,000 cubic feet sanctuary to less than 1-1/2 seconds to enhance speech intelligibility. The central ceiling is hard-surfaced to retain the feeling of acoustical presence for pastor and congregation.

The organ loudspeakers are recessed in the forward wall. The speech reinforcement system consists of a high central forward cluster assisted by upper balcony projectors and lower balcony overhead loudspeakers with appropriate delay. Microphone outlets in choir, podium and orchestra pit provide full audio coverage for all functions.

Initial musical and religious events were an acoustical success. Speech intelligibility is excellent, with minor central cluster "hot spots" due to the use of only three horn projectors *vs* the plan for four. Air system noise is caused by supply air outlet dampers installed contrary to recommendations. These deficiencies will be corrected.

GRACE BRETHREN CHURCH
COLUMBUS, OHIO
COMPLETED 1983

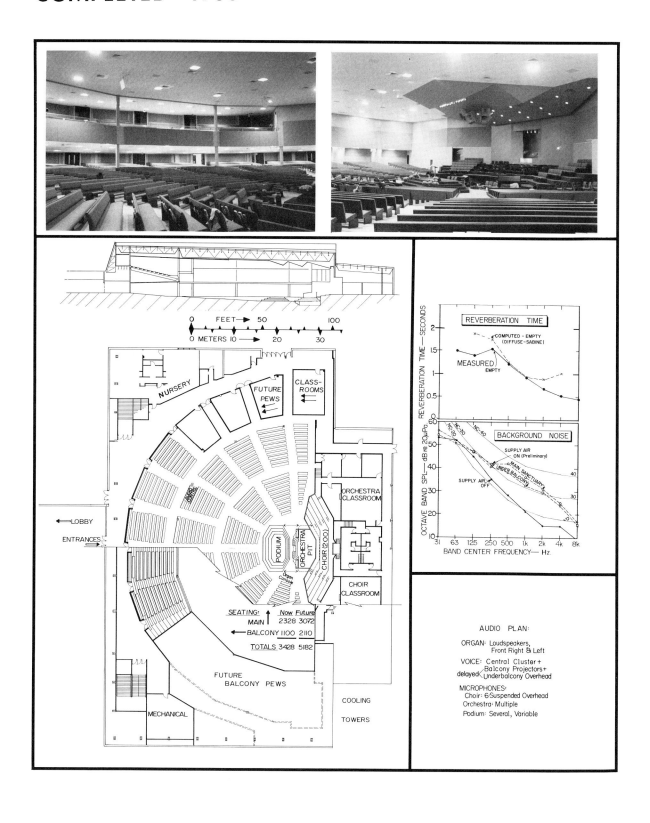

O FEET ➤ 50   100
O METERS 10 ➤ 20   30

NURSERY

FUTURE PEWS

CLASS-ROOMS

ORCHESTRA CLASSROOM

◄— LOBBY

ENTRANCES

PODIUM

ORCHESTRA PIT

CHOIR (200)

Organ Console

CHOIR CLASSROOM

SEATING: Now Future
MAIN   2328 3072
◄—BALCONY   1100 2110
TOTALS   3428 5182

FUTURE BALCONY PEWS

COOLING

MECHANICAL

TOWERS

REVERBERATION TIME

COMPUTED - EMPTY
(DIFFUSE-SABINE)

MEASURED
EMPTY

REVERBERATION TIME—SECONDS

BACKGROUND NOISE

OCTAVE BAND SPL—dB re 20μPa

NC-50
NC-40
NC-30
NC-20

SUPPLY AIR ON (Preliminary)

MAIN SANCTUARY

UNDER BALCONY

SUPPLY AIR OFF

31 63 125 250 500 1k 2k 4k 8k
BAND CENTER FREQUENCY— Hz.

AUDIO PLAN:

ORGAN: Loudspeakers,
        Front Right & Left

VOICE: Central Cluster +
        Balcony Projectors +
delayed Underbalcony Overhead

MICROPHONES:
  Choir: 6 Suspended Overhead
  Orchestra: Multiple
  Podium: Several, Variable

ST. BRENDAN CHURCH
COLUMBUS, OHIO

COMPLETED: June 1981

OWNER: Catholic Diocese of Columbus

ARCHITECT: Meacham & Apel

ACOUSTICAL CONSULTANT: Angelo J. Campanella, ACCULAB

CONTRACTOR: Cody-Zeigler, Inc.

OTHER CONSULTANTS: Heapy Engineering (Elec & Mech)
                                    Lantz, Jones & Nebraska (struct)

TOTAL CONSTRUCTION COST: $600,000 (building only)

St. Brendan Church is part of a 23-acre religious, 1 through 8 educational facility. The nave is over 6000 square feet, air-conditioned, and seats 700 plus a choir of 25. All pews are wooden and the floor is polished aggregate. The ceiling and sidewalls are gypsum board. The forward walls are solid local stone, externally buttressed. Sound diffusion by the polygonal plan and vaulted ceiling avoids echoes and enhances music. Sound absorption by carpeting over rear entrances and sidewalls limits empty room reverberation time to less than 3 seconds.

The Humpe organ (Richmond, Ohio) comprises nine ranks, two manuals and pedals. The speech reinforcement system consists of four directional loudspeakers finished to match the stone wall. Preset electronic controls are switched on by the pastor when needed. A wireless microphone is used by the pastor, with fixed microphones for lay readings and choir.

From the outset, soprano voice and organ renditions were brilliant. Subsequent acoustical efforts have been aimed at improving speech intelligibility. With this wide-angle seating, intelligibility without reinforcement is possible only with the raised voice. An equalized nave sound system of concealed ceiling loudspeakers was mainly unintelligible due to excess reverberation and was disconnected. Directional horns were mounted in pairs on the forward wall and directed to the pews, providing good intelligibility with third octave equalization. This sound is reproduced in the meeting room, narthex, sacristy and rectory.

ST. BRENDAN CHURCH
COLUMBUS, OHIO
COMPLETED - 1981

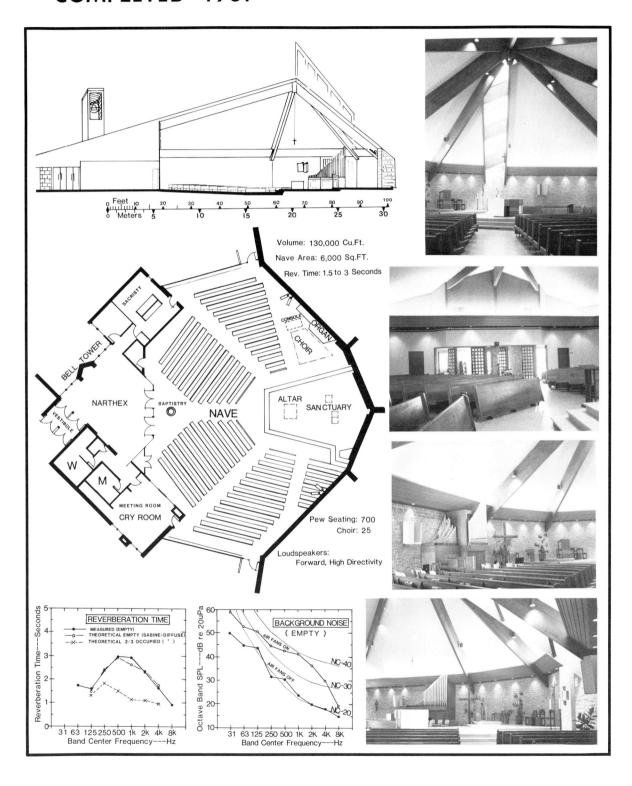

Volume: 130,000 Cu.Ft.

Nave Area: 6,000 Sq.FT.

Rev. Time: 1.5 to 3 Seconds

Pew Seating: 700

Choir: 25

Loudspeakers:
Forward, High Directivity

REVERBERATION TIME

MEASURED (EMPTY)
THEORETICAL EMPTY (SABINE-DIFFUSE)
THEORETICAL 2/3 OCCUPIED (" ")

Reverberation Time---Seconds

Band Center Frequency---Hz

BACKGROUND NOISE
(EMPTY)

AIR FANS ON

AIR FANS OFF

NC-40

NC-30

NC-20

Octave Band SPL----dB re 20uPa

Band Center Frequency---Hz

FIRST UNITED METHODIST CHURCH
CORVALLIS, OREGON

RENOVATION COMPLETED:	1979
ARCHITECT:	Callahan & MacCollin Salem, Oregon
ACOUSTICAL CONSULTANT:	Daly Engineering Company Beaverton, Oregon
ENGINEER:	Long, Maxwell & Associates Tigard, Oregon (mechanical)
TOTAL RENOVATION COST:	$1,000,000

The First United Methodist Church is located in the college town of Corvallis directly across the street from Oregon State University. The church has a volume of 173,000 cubic feet and a total floor area of approximately 4400 square feet.

In 1977, for the second time in 40 years, the sanctuary of the church was destroyed by fire. Prior to this last fire, a brief study was made of the sanctuary in an attempt to determine the source or sources of some complaints from the congregation. A problem with non-uniform low frequency absorption was identified in the room. In an attempt to prevent this problem in the renovated sanctuary, low frequency absorbing panels that blended in with the natural walls were used on each side of the side-wall windows. As can be seen from the reverberation time measurements made in the restored sanctuary, the low frequency absorption is higher than it should be for optimum speech or music conditions but this was done with the above purpose in mind.

Prior to the restoration, the choir was located in a narrow area behind the chancel and between two organ lofts. The organ played into this choir area. This proved very unsatisfactory for two reasons. First, the choir had difficulty hearing the service as well as themselves. Second, the projection of both choir and organ music out into the main seating area was poor. This was especially evident in the balcony where the sound was simply not heard. After the fire, $125,000 was spent on a new organ. The chancel area was opened up and elaborate reflectors installed on the sides of the chancel area to improve projection into the sanctuary.

60

FIRST UNITED METHODIST CHURCH
CORVALLIS, OREGON U.S.A.
RENOVATION COMPLETED - 1979

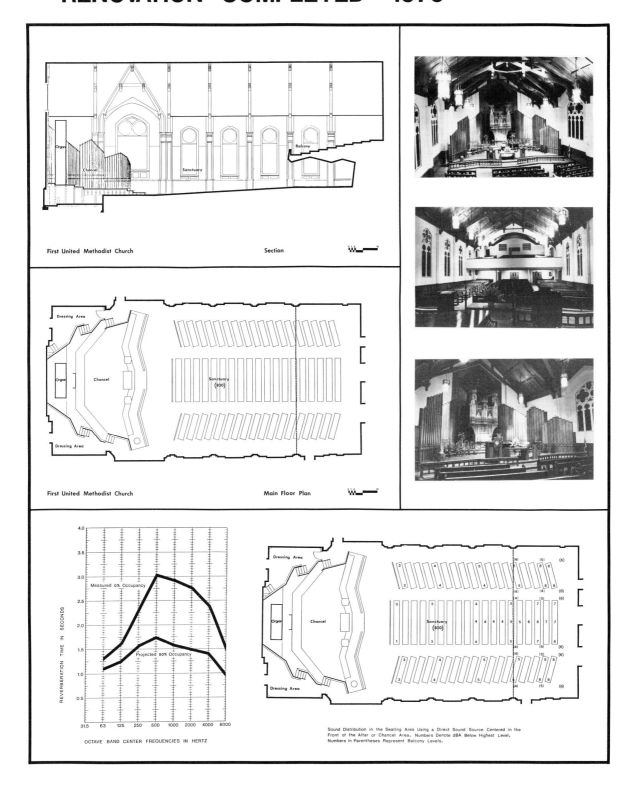

First United Methodist Church   Section

First United Methodist Church   Main Floor Plan

OCTAVE BAND CENTER FREQUENCIES IN HERTZ

Sound Distribution in the Seating Area Using a Direct Sound Source Centered in the Front of the Altar or Chancel Area. Numbers Denote dBA Below Highest Level. Numbers in Parentheses Represent Balcony Levels.

UNITED CHURCH OF CHRIST
FOREST GROVE, OREGON

CONSTRUCTION COMPLETED: 1978

ARCHITECT: Zimmer, Gunsul, Frasca
                                Portland, Oregon

ACOUSTICAL CONSULTANT: Daly Engineering Company
                                Beaverton, Oregon

ENGINEERS: Keith Kruchek
                                Portland, Oregon (mechanical)
                                Langton, Mehlig
                                Portland, Oregon (electrical)

TOTAL CONSTRUCTION COST: $550,000

The United Church of Christ is located in the small college town of Forest Grove, directly across the street from Pacific University. The 117,000 cubic foot church, with a total floor area of approximately 3600 square feet, is primarily used for music-oriented church services and small concerts.

The position of the chancel area, combined with the shape of the room, presented some problems in obtaining good sound distribution through the room. To enhance the sound distribution, the wall behind the chancel area was given a slightly convex shape. At one corner, the walls were placed 4 degrees out of square to prevent the establishment of adverse tangential modes of room response.

The shape of the room and the placement of the stained glass windows also made it difficult to obtain uniform absorption throughout the room. The contrast of the unique wood truss system of the ceiling to the stark white gypsum board walls also presented problems in selecting an absorptive material that could be used throughout the room. It was decided to leave the lower walls of gypsum board for low frequency absorption and to introduce uniformly spaced wood slats with an absorptive backing in the wood ceiling area to absorb mid and high frequencies. While this admittedly does not represent uniform absorption, it seemed to be the most acceptable condition that fell within the design constraints.

UNITED CHURCH OF CHRIST
FOREST GROVE, OREGON U.S.A.
CONSTRUCTION COMPLETED - 1978

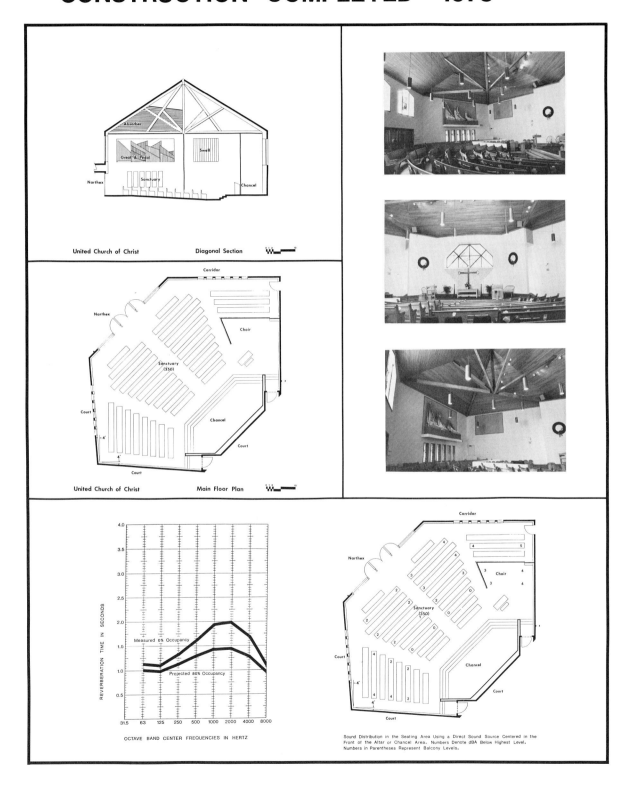

United Church of Christ   Diagonal Section

United Church of Christ   Main Floor Plan

OCTAVE BAND CENTER FREQUENCIES IN HERTZ

Measured 0% Occupancy

Projected 80% Occupancy

Sound Distribution in the Seating Area Using a Direct Sound Source Centered in the Front of the Altar or Chancel Area. Numbers Denote dBA Below Highest Level. Numbers in Parentheses Represent Balcony Levels.

FIRST CHURCH OF THE NAZARENE
PORTLAND, OREGON

CONSTRUCTION COMPLETED: 1980

ARCHITECT: Daniel, Mann, Johnson and
                              Mendenhall
                            Portland, Oregon

ACOUSTICAL CONSULTANT: Daly Engineering Company
                            Beaverton, Oregon

ENGINEERS: C. W. Timmer
                            Beaverton, Oregon (mechanical)

                            Langton, Mehlig
                            Portland, Oregon (electrical)

TOTAL CONSTRUCTION COST: $3,000,000

The First Church of the Nazarene is located in the wooded west hills of Portland. The 350,000 cubic foot church, with a total floor area of approximately 14,500 square feet, was designed for music-oriented church services and also to be used for large concerts.

Approximately one year after being completed, the roof of the sanctuary collapsed. Luckily, no one was in the sanctuary at the time. It has since been rebuilt to the original specifications.

An interesting feature of the sanctuary is the baptistry mezzanine. There is a pod with two large doors above the choir platform that can be opened exposing a full-immersion baptistry to the entire sanctuary. When closed, which is the normal position, the surfaces give desired sound diffusion.

The seats were chosen to be fairly highly absorbing to minimize the difference in the reverberation times under varying occupancy conditions.

There was extensive shaping of the side walls and ceiling to achieve the fairly uniform sound distribution throughout the sanctuary.

To reduce adverse reflections, the concave back wall of the lower seating area and balcony area was covered with uniformly spaced wooden slats with an absorptive backing.

FIRST CHURCH OF THE NAZARENE
PORTLAND, OREGON U.S.A.
CONSTRUCTION COMPLETED - 1980

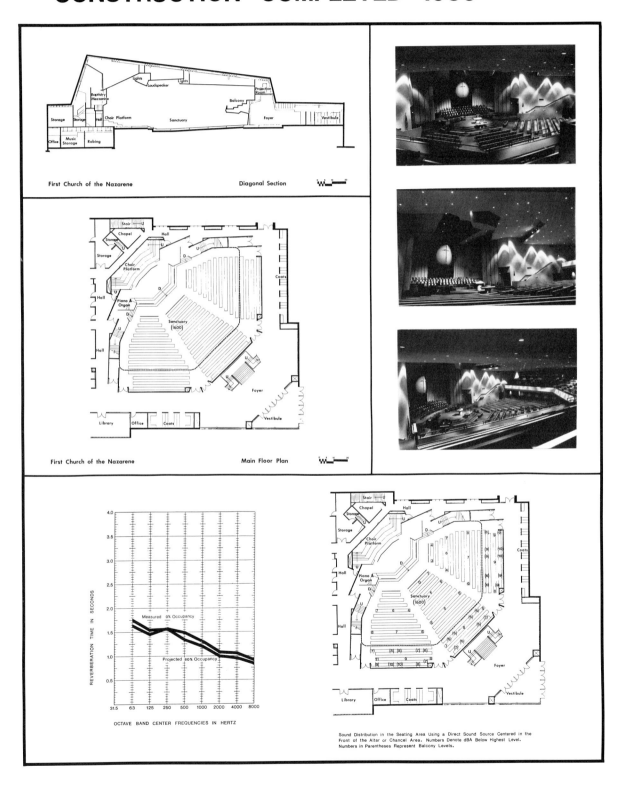

First Church of the Nazarene   Diagonal Section

First Church of the Nazarene   Main Floor Plan

REVERBERATION TIME IN SECONDS

Measured 0% Occupancy

Projected 80% Occupancy

OCTAVE BAND CENTER FREQUENCIES IN HERTZ

Sound Distribution in the Seating Area Using a Direct Sound Source Centered in the Front of the Altar or Chancel Area. Numbers Denote dBA Below Highest Level. Numbers in Parentheses Represent Balcony Levels.

SAINT THERESE CATHOLIC CHURCH
PORTLAND, OREGON

CONSTRUCTION COMPLETED: 1983

ARCHITECT: Zaik/Miller
                               Portland, Oregon

ACOUSTICAL CONSULTANT: Daly Engineering Company
                               Beaverton, Oregon

ENGINEERS: Morrison, Funatake, Inouye,
                                  Andrews
                               Portland, Oregon
                               (mechanical & electrical)

TOTAL CONSTRUCTION COST: $785,000

Saint Therese Catholic Church is located in east Portland. The 206,000 cubic foot church, with a total floor area of approximately 6800 square feet, is used almost exclusively for church services.

It was the desire of the congregation for the room to perform well acoustically with the installation of a newly purchased organ. The shape of the ceiling of the church and the extensive use of wood throughout lent themselves well to making the room respond well to organ music. The low frequency absorption characteristics of the gypsum board panels used extensively thoughout the church was eliminated by applying double sheets of the panels everywhere to stiffen them.

The application of highly absorbing panels in the tower area above the altar was used to eliminate problems of the tower acting as a coupled chamber. The only other real absorbing material in the sanctuary is the fairly lightly absorbing carpet applied in the aisles and altar area.

The central main beam bisecting the sanctuary and the side beams radiating out from it and away from the altar area aid in obtaining good sound distribution throughout the room.

The crying room was acoustically isolated from the main sanctuary by double pane windows, slanted from top to bottom to minimize adverse light reflections to the occupants of the room.

SAINT THERESE CATHOLIC CHURCH
PORTLAND, OREGON U.S.A.
CONSTRUCTION COMPLETED - 1983

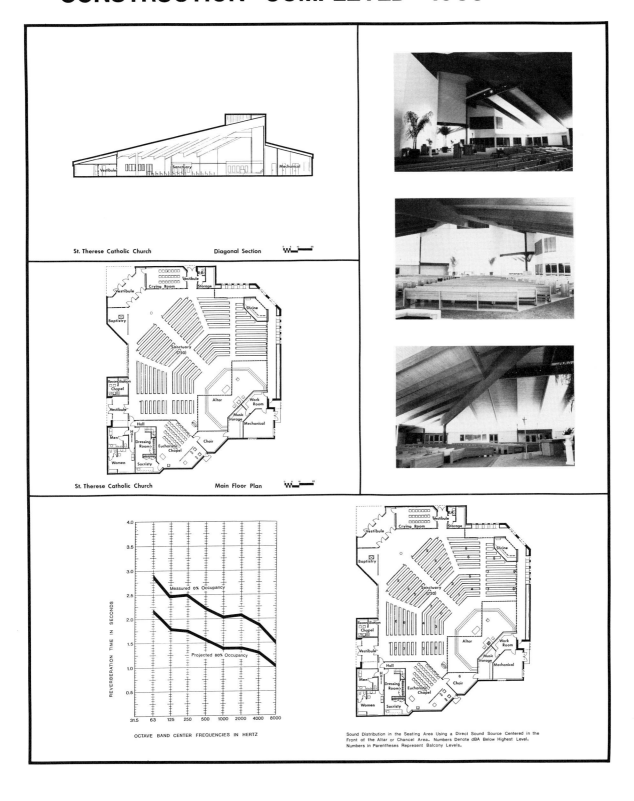

St. Therese Catholic Church Diagonal Section

St. Therese Catholic Church Main Floor Plan

REVERBERATION TIME IN SECONDS

Measured 0% Occupancy

Projected 80% Occupancy

OCTAVE BAND CENTER FREQUENCIES IN HERTZ

Sound Distribution in the Seating Area Using a Direct Sound Source Centered in the Front of the Altar or Chancel Area. Numbers Denote dBA Below Highest Level. Numbers in Parentheses Represent Balcony Levels.

HOLY TRINITY SERBIAN ORTHODOX CHURCH
ALIQUIPPA, PENNSYLVANIA

COMPLETED: 1968

ARCHITECT: John V. Tomich
                                   Aliquippa, Pennsylvania

ACOUSTICAL CONSULTANT: Jaffe Acoustics, Inc.
                                   Norwalk, Connecticut

Unique design criteria dictated an aesthetic which was reminiscent of a more Mediterranean approach to style and materials. Its success has been evidenced by two awards: The A.I.A. Pennsylvania Chapter Award for Design Excellence and the American Concrete Institute Pittsburgh Chapter Award for Concrete Design.

The acoustic design required control of reverberation in a space with relatively large volume and hard reflective boundary surfaces. The results of acoustic treatments yielded a reverberation of 2.1 seconds. This has proven to be acceptable for many Eastern Orthodox rites. The space is especially responsive during music presentations.

SERBIAN ORTHODOX CHURCH
ALIQUIPPA, PENNSYLVANIA
CONSTRUCTION COMPLETED — 1968

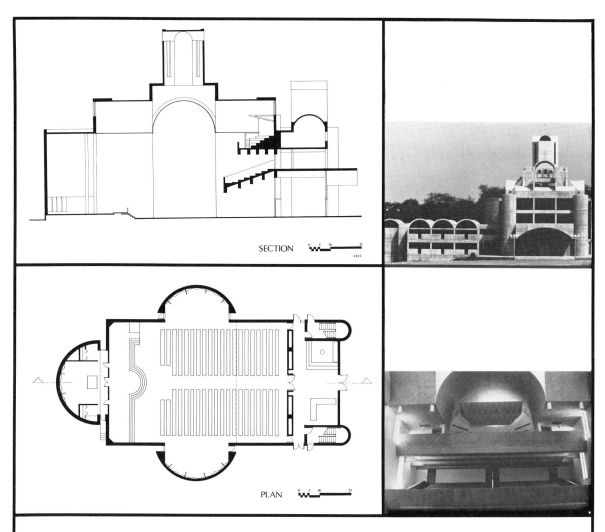

SECTION

PLAN

ACOUSTIC DATA

VOLUME OF HALL – V : **291,000** ft^3

SEATS IN AUDIENCE – N_A : **630** seats

AUDIENCE SEATING AREA – S_A : **4780** ft^2

PODIUM AREA – S_P : **630** ft^2

REVERBERATION TIME : **2.1** sec.
Mid – frequency

INITIAL TIME DELAY GAP : **18** msec.

$S_T = S_A + S_P$: **5410** ft^2

S_A/N_A : **7.5** ft^2/pers.

V/S_T : **54**

TEMPLE ISRAEL
MEMPHIS, TENNESSEE

COMPLETED:	1976
OWNER:	Temple Israel
ARCHITECT:	Gassner Nathan & Partners
ACOUSTICAL CONSULTANT:	Newcomb & Boyd Atlanta, Georgia
ENGINEERS	Griffith C. Burr, Inc. Mechanical/Electrical
	Kenworthy Scott and Associates Structural
TOTAL CONSTRUCTION COST:	$4,840,000

The Temple Israel was designed to recreate the intimacy of the Temple's 60 year old Byzantine structure in the inner city. The facility includes a 250 seat chapel and a larger multipurpose presentation hall in addition to the 1350 seat sanctuary.

To provide reflective surfaces behind the Bema, the Ark is enclosed with oak over oak plywood, with bronze-coated aluminum doors. The stone mosaic of the Wings of the Cherubim provides additional reflective surfaces.

Due to the semi-circular layout, the farthest listener is no more than 15 rows (52 feet) from the Bema. A distributed sound system was installed for sound reinforcement in the sanctuary. The reverberation time in the sanctuary is intended to provide good speech intelligibility throughout the space without excessively compromising the sound of the choir and pipe organ.

TEMPLE ISRAEL
MEMPHIS, TENNESSEE
1976

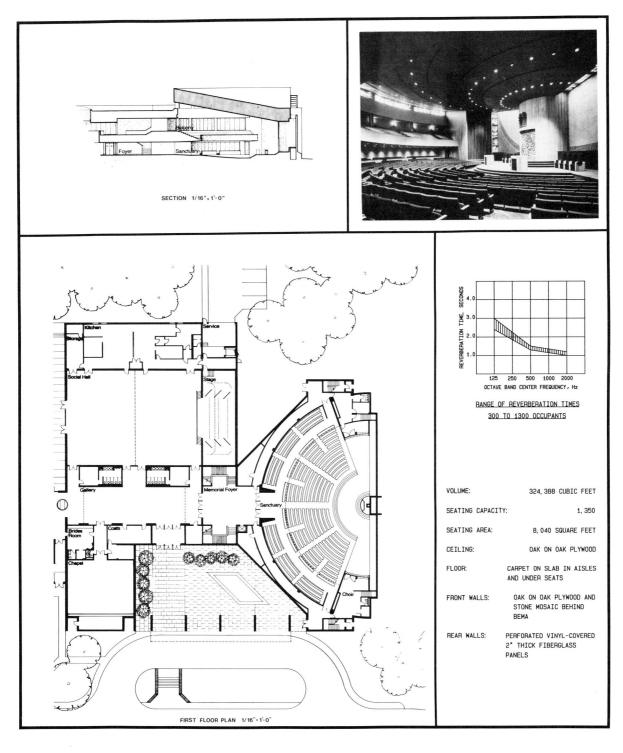

SECTION 1/16" = 1'-0"

REVERBERATION TIME, SECONDS

125   250   500   1000   2000
OCTAVE BAND CENTER FREQUENCY, Hz

RANGE OF REVERBERATION TIMES
300 TO 1300 OCCUPANTS

FIRST FLOOR PLAN 1/16" = 1'-0"

VOLUME:	324,388 CUBIC FEET
SEATING CAPACITY:	1,350
SEATING AREA:	8,040 SQUARE FEET
CEILING:	OAK ON OAK PLYWOOD
FLOOR:	CARPET ON SLAB IN AISLES AND UNDER SEATS
FRONT WALLS:	OAK ON OAK PLYWOOD AND STONE MOSAIC BEHIND BEMA
REAR WALLS:	PERFORATED VINYL-COVERED 2" THICK FIBERGLASS PANELS

LOVERS LANE UNITED METHODIST CHURCH
DALLAS, TEXAS

COMPLETED:	1976
ARCHITECT:	Thomas Stanley Dallas, Texas
INTERIOR DESIGN:	Rambusch Associates New York
ACOUSTICAL CONSULTANT:	Joiner-Pelton-Rose, Inc., Dallas, Texas

Splayed stained glass sidewalls and pyramidal plaster ceiling elements were introduced to increase diffusion in a traditional rectangular enclosure. Choir and organ are in the balcony; a reversed antiphonal organ is located on a concealed lift on the chancel platform.

Noise and vibration from a large HVAC plant below the nave are effectively isolated from both the sanctuary and the adjacent choir practice spaces.

The client and architect did not want a loudspeaker cluster hanging in the way of the stained glass at the front of the church. To preserve the visual impact of the design, a distributed pew-back system was selected. The operator is located on the main sanctuary floor, necessitating a delayed monitor signal.

The result is a live, light, airy design with simple lines and materials, and good articulation of reinforced speech.

LOVERS LANE UNITED METHODIST CHURCH
DALLAS, TEXAS
COMPLETED 1976

JOINER-PELTON-ROSE, INC

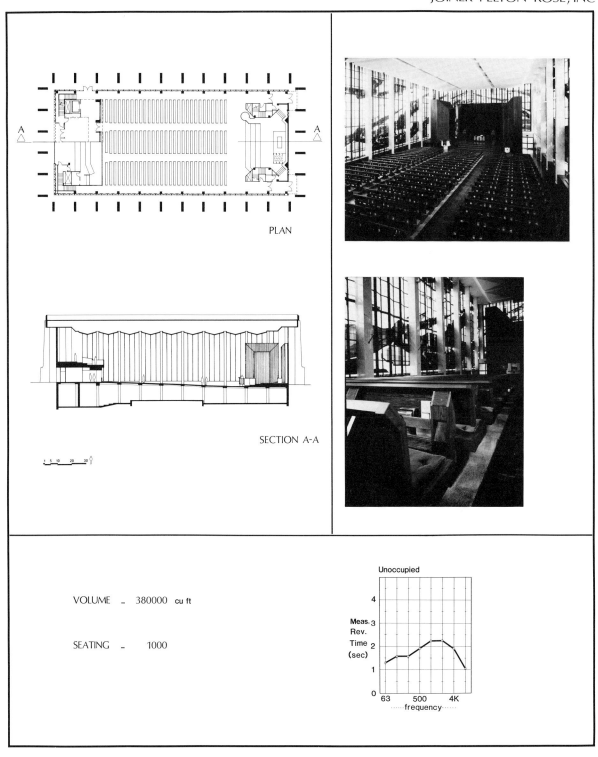

PLAN

SECTION A-A

1 5 10   20   30

VOLUME — 380000 cu ft

SEATING — 1000

Unoccupied

Meas. Rev. Time (sec)

4
3
2
1
0

63   500   4K

frequency

CLEAR LAKE PRESBYTERIAN CHURCH
HOUSTON, TEXAS

COMPLETED:	1983
ARCHITECT:	Clovis Heimsath Associates,Inc. Fayetteville, Texas
ACOUSTICAL CONSULTANT:	Joiner-Pelton-Rose, Inc. Dallas, Texas
PASTOR	The Reverend Jay Cannon

The sanctuary is a comfortably traditional, rectangular room with a painted wood deck ceiling, white plasterboard walls and upholstered pews. Carpet is installed in the chancel, under pews, and in the aisles and music area. The organ by Casavant Freres of Ste. Hyacinthe, Quebec is located next to the choir. Volume ratio is 326 cubic feet per seat. A small chapel at the rear can be used for overflow space.

The design has a rustic Southwestern flavor throughout. A section of stained glass throws a stream of colored light down the center aisle to the very simple pulpit. Directly behind the pulpit, the white partitions are designed to enhance the regional feel of the sanctuary. The design is intensely dramatic, while maintaining a subdued reverence.

Care was taken to ensure low noise and vibration levels from air-handling equipment, both mechanically and architecturally. The design goal for the completed sanctuary was NC 25 - 30.

Existing sound system components were reused for the new sanctuary, with the speakers located on a beam over the pulpit area. The design allows for even coverage with no hot spots.

CLEAR LAKE PRESBYTERIAN CHURCH
HOUSTON, TEXAS
COMPLETED 1983

JOINER-PELTON-ROSE, INC

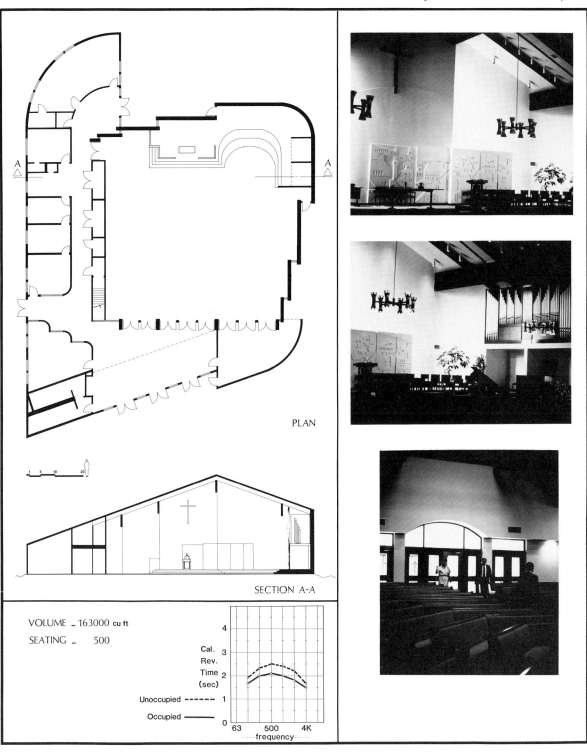

PLAN

SECTION A-A

VOLUME _ 163000 cu ft

SEATING _ 500

Cal.
Rev.
Time
(sec)

4

3

2

1

0

Unoccupied -----

Occupied ———

63   500   4K

·······frequency·······

PARK PLACE BAPTIST CHURCH
HOUSTON, TEXAS

RENOVATION COMPLETED: 1983

ARCHITECT: Ben F. Greenwood

ACOUSTICAL CONSULTANT: Hoover Keith & Bruce Inc.
                                     Houston, Texas

COST: $50,000

Park Place Baptist Church was built in 1964 as a worship facility with seating for 1500 on the main floor and 1000 in the balcony. The sound system described here is the fourth to be installed since the sanctuary was completed.

The church is used almost exclusively for worship services, but choral presentations and community events such as graduation ceremonies are occasionally held there.

The purpose of the acoustical renovation was to improve sound coverage and speech intelligibility for the listeners, provide more operational flexibility to support larger choir programs, and eliminate an echo which was distracting to persons on stage because of its long delay (about 250 milliseconds).

The sound system was upgraded using constant-directivity horns in a single central cluster; left and right-channel effects speakers were added to augment musical productions. The mixing console was moved from an enclosed control room to the front row of the balcony. The echo was eliminated and the reverberation time decreased slightly by the addition of 1260 square feet of fabric-covered absorptive material to the balcony face and rear wall.

PARK PLACE BAPTIST CHURCH
HOUSTON, TEXAS
RENOVATION COMPLETED 1983

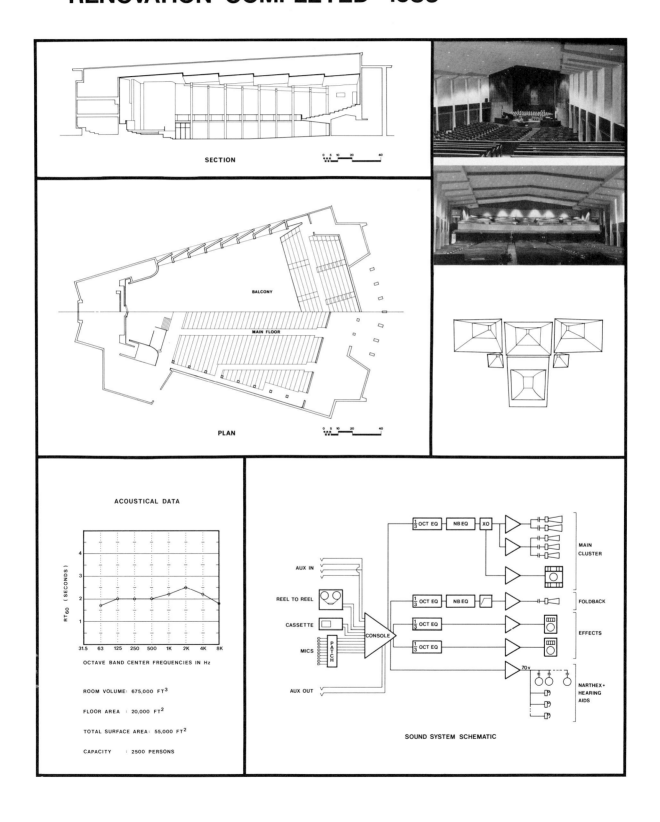

SECTION

0 5 10 20 40

BALCONY

MAIN FLOOR

PLAN

0 5 10 20 40

ACOUSTICAL DATA

RT$_{60}$ (SECONDS)

31.5 63 125 250 500 1K 2K 4K 8K

OCTAVE BAND CENTER FREQUENCIES IN Hz

ROOM VOLUME: 675,000 FT^3

FLOOR AREA : 20,000 FT^2

TOTAL SURFACE AREA: 55,000 FT^2

CAPACITY : 2500 PERSONS

AUX IN

REEL TO REEL

CASSETTE

MICS

AUX OUT

PATCH

CONSOLE

$\frac{1}{3}$ OCT EQ   NB EQ   XO

$\frac{1}{3}$ OCT EQ   NB EQ

$\frac{1}{3}$ OCT EQ

$\frac{1}{3}$ OCT EQ

70v

MAIN CLUSTER

FOLDBACK

EFFECTS

NARTHEX + HEARING AIDS

SOUND SYSTEM SCHEMATIC

UNIVERSITY PRESBYTERIAN CHURCH
SEATTLE, WASHINGTON

RENOVATION COMPLETED: 1982

OWNER: University Presbyterian Church

ACOUSTICAL CONSULTANT: Towne, Richards & Chaudiere, Inc.
                               Seattle, Washington

SOUND SYSTEM CONTRACTOR: Electrocom
                               Seattle, Washington

COST OF RENOVATION: $35,000

The traditional "shoebox" nave with 1350 seating capacity, including a balcony, has an unoccupied reverberation time on the order of 2 seconds. This drops to around 1.7 seconds with an occupancy of 1200.

Absorption in the nave is limited to pew cushions and carpet in the aisles. Musical performance was deemed excellent but an antiquated sound system had to be replaced to provide good speech intelligibility uniformly throughout the seating areas while maintaining directional realism.

The new sound system utilizes a single-source array consisting of two $60° \times 40°$ constant-directivity horns and a bass unit. These are located above the sanctuary and operate in combination with time-delayed, distributed speakers in the balcony, under the balcony and in the Narthex. A $90° \times 40°$ horn in the array provides coverage of the sanctuary area. The system has independent mixing capabilities for sound reinforcement and record/broadcast of services.

A portable remote volume-control unit is provided for the sound reinforcement function to permit control from the balcony or the sound booth. Extensive use is made of wireless microphones.

UNIVERSITY PRESBYTERIAN CHURCH
SEATTLE, WASHINGTON
RENOVATION COMPLETED 1982

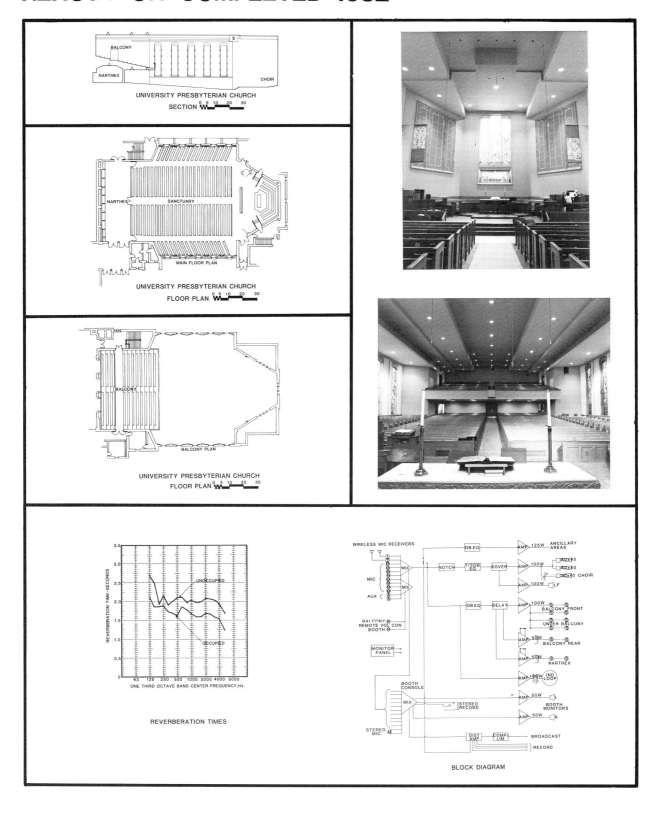

GLAD TIDINGS PENTECOSTAL CHURCH
VICTORIA, BRITISH COLUMBIA, CANADA

COMPLETED: 1978

ARCHITECT: Vern H. Delgatty
                                    Vancouver, Canada

ACOUSTICAL CONSULTANT: Paoletti/Lewitz/Associates,Inc.
                                    San Francisco, California

MECHANICAL ENGINEER: Territorial Projects Ltd.
                                    Vancouver, Canada

ELECTRICAL ENGINEER: Perelco Design Ltd.
                                    Vancouver, Canada

This collaboration between architect and church leaders has led to a very interesting and aesthetically pleasing structure. Music plays a very important part in the Pentecostal worship service. Hence, in addition to liturgy, sermon, and spoken word, the altar area is used for choral groups and various musical performances ranging from piano or organ accompaniment to a small band.

The acoustical environment is similar in many ways to that of a multi-purpose performing arts facility. Important sound projecting surfaces close to the sound source are sound-reflective. They are also splayed to project sound towards the congregation and to prevent detrimental acoustical characteristics such as echoes. The surfaces surrounding the congregation are also sound reflective to reinforce the singing and chanting of the congregation during the worship service.

The high-quality sound reinforcement system provides recording, monitoring and production-communication capabilities. The sound system operator is located on the mezzanine at the rear with the sound console, tape recorder, electronic controls and playback equipment.

Large windows introduce natural light and enhance viewing both into and out of the church. The use of reflective glass for the front wall of the church, extensive planters within the church, and exposed structure produces an inspiring building for worship. The acoustical design complements the architecture and helps support the emotional and religious experience of the congregation.

GLAD TIDINGS PENTECOSTAL CHURCH
VICTORIA B.C., CANADA
COMPLETED 1978

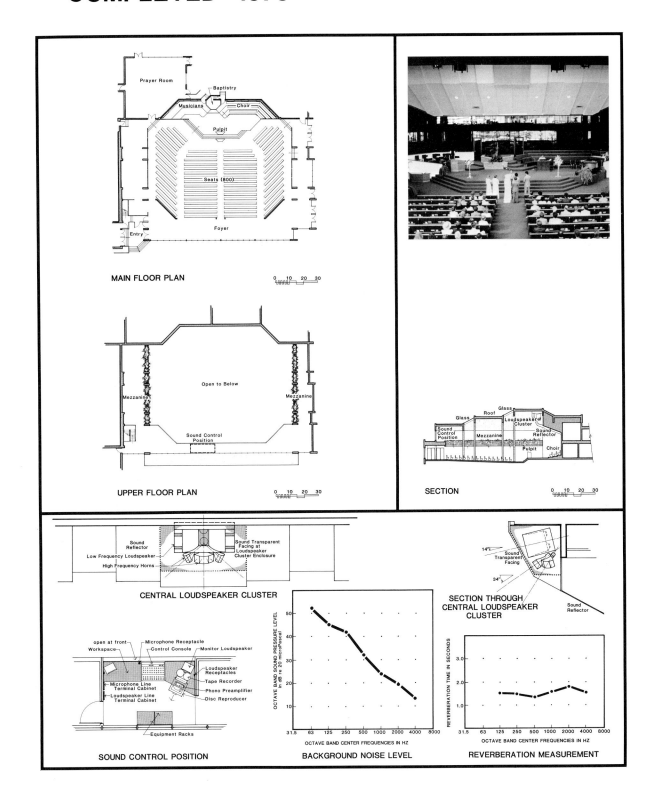

SANTUARIO de GUADALUPE
MONTERREY, MEXICO

COMPLETED: 1983

ARCHITECT: Pedro Vasquez, Antonio Muguerza
                                    and Juan Najera

ACOUSTICAL CONSULTANT: Joiner-Pelton-Rose, Inc.
                                    Dallas, Texas

The sanctuary consists of a pyramidal space approximately 140 feet square and 88 feet high at the peak. Simple wood pews seat 2500, for a volume ratio of 235 cubic feet per person. The floor, altar, cross, and lower sidewalls are polished stone. The four sloped sides consist of a thin, perforated inner steel skin with locally produced 6-pound density rockwool to absorb reflected sound energy. An array of 57 manila ship hawsers is suspended as a unique backdrop behind the altar area. Large stained-glass windows fill the triangular slots between the inclined roof planes.

A central cluster with controlled-directivity, high-frequency horns was designed for installation behind an acoustically transparent area in the Imagen, a screen bearing the image of the Virgin.

The Sanctuary is air-conditioned; HVAC noise isolation was obtained by custom-designed attenuation elements for local manufacture and installation.

SANTUARIO DE GUADALUPE
MONTERREY, MEXICO
COMPLETED 1983

JOINER-PELTON-ROSE, INC

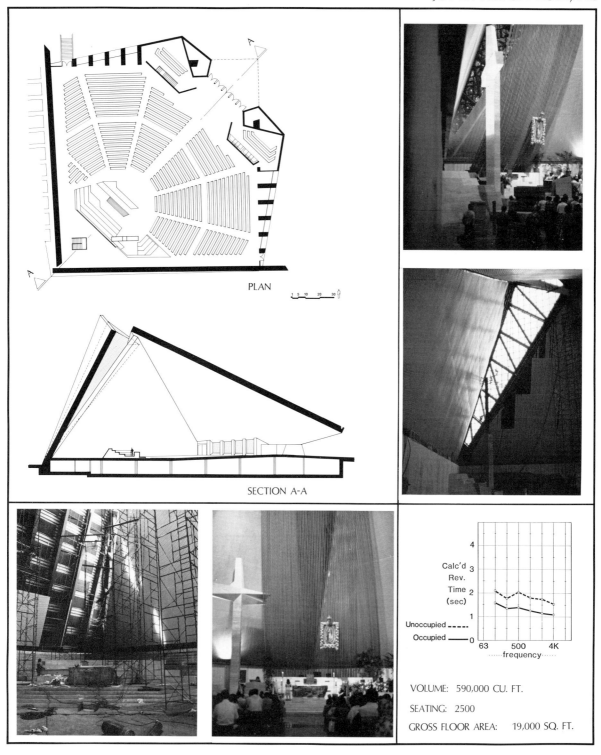

PLAN

SECTION A-A

Calc'd Rev. Time (sec)

Unoccupied ----
Occupied ——

frequency

63   500   4K

VOLUME: 590,000 CU. FT.

SEATING: 2500

GROSS FLOOR AREA: 19,000 SQ. FT.

THE SANCTUARY OF SHINJI-SHUMEI-KAI, SACRED GARDEN
SHIGA, JAPAN

COMPLETED:	1983
OWNER:	Shinji-Shumei-Kai
ARCHITECT:	Minoru Yamasaki
ACOUSTICAL CONSULTANT:	Minoru Nagata & Associates Tokyo, Japan
COST:	$62,500,000

The Sacred Garden Shiga was constructed as the general headquarters of Shinji-Shu-mei-Kai in Shigaraki, about 50 kilometers southeast of Kyoto. The sanctuary has a volume of 87,000 cubic meters, accommodates 5000 seats, and is intended for various types of musical performance as well as for religious events.

The main theme of the acoustical study was the design and arrangement of absorbing structures and the design of the loudspeaker system to provide good speech intelligibility in such a huge and reverberant space.

Mainly for aesthetic reasons, the ceiling and walls of the sanctuary, except the rear wall, are finished with sound reflective materials. Sound absorbing area remains only in the carpeted floor with audience and the rear wall.

A central cluster was designed as a main system to cover the whole seating area. In addition, the seat-back system with a loudspeaker for every two seats was provided to give special emphasis to religious events.

The central cluster was designed to meet the following requirements:
1) a Q factor to get sufficient direct-to-reverberant energy ratio,
2) directivity in horizontal plane to get "% Disturbance" less than 10% due to side wall reflections,
3) directivity in the vertical plane (microphone direction) to give stable operation against feedback.

The acoustical measurements show that good speech intelligibility is realized as expected. Since the opening, the sanctuary has acquired a reputation for good acoustics, both for orchestral concerts and organ recitals.

THE SANCTUARY OF SHINJI-SHUMEI-KAI, SACRED GARDEN
SHIGA, JAPAN
COMPLETED — 1983

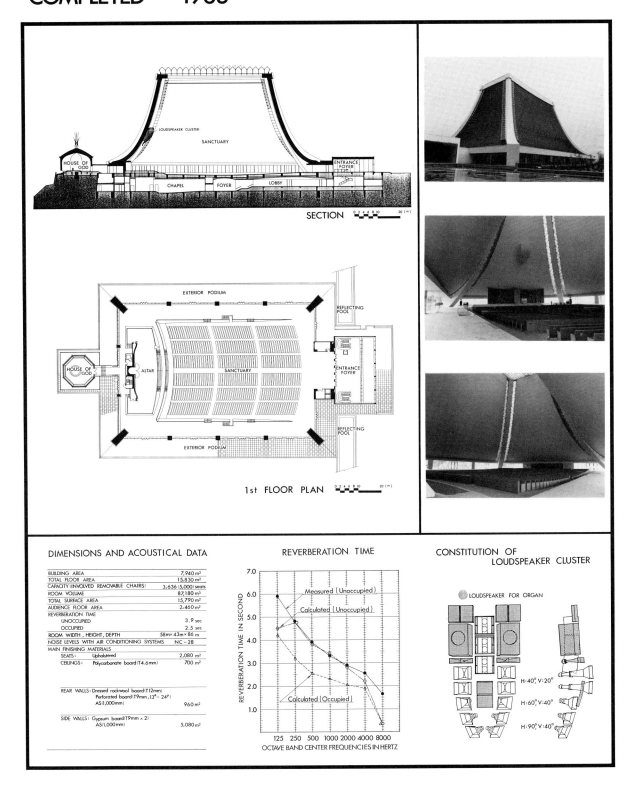

SECTION

LOUDSPEAKER CLUSTER
SANCTUARY
HOUSE OF GOD
CHAPEL   FOYER   LOBBY
ENTRANCE FOYER

1st FLOOR PLAN

EXTERIOR PODIUM
REFLECTING POOL
HOUSE OF GOD
ALTAR
SANCTUARY
ENTRANCE FOYER
REFLECTING POOL
EXTERIOR PODIUM

DIMENSIONS AND ACOUSTICAL DATA

BUILDING AREA	7,940 m²
TOTAL FLOOR AREA	15,830 m²
CAPACITY (INVOLVED REMOVABLE CHAIRS)	3,636 (5,000) seats
ROOM VOLUME	87,180 m³
TOTAL SURFACE AREA	15,790 m²
AUDIENCE FLOOR AREA	2,460 m²
REVERBERATION TIME	
UNOCCUPIED	3.9 sec
OCCUPIED	2.5 sec
ROOM WIDTH, HEIGHT, DEPTH	58m×43m×86 m
NOISE LEVELS WITH AIR CONDITIONING SYSTEMS	NC – 28
MAIN FINISHING MATERIALS	
SEATS: Upholstered	2,080 m²
CEILINGS: Polycarbonate board (T4.6mm)	700 m²

REAR WALLS: Dressed rockwool board (T12mm)	
Perforated board (T9mm, 13°– 24°)	
AS (1,000mm)	960 m²
SIDE WALLS: Gypsum board (T9mm × 2)	
AS (1,000mm)	5,080 m²

REVERBERATION TIME

Measured (Unoccupied)
Calculated (Unoccupied)
Calculated (Occupied)

REVERBERATION TIME IN SECOND

125 250 500 1000 2000 4000 8000
OCTAVE BAND CENTER FREQUENCIES IN HERTZ

CONSTITUTION OF LOUDSPEAKER CLUSTER

LOUDSPEAKER FOR ORGAN

H:40°, V:20°
H:60°, V:40°
H:90°, V:40°

ST. ANSELM'S PRIORY
TOKYO, JAPAN

RENOVATION COMPLETED: 1983

OWNER: Benedictine Mission

ARCHITECT: Antonin Raymond

ACOUSTICAL CONSULTANT: Minoru Nagata & Associates
                               Tokyo, Japan

The church of St. Anselm's Priory is located near the JNR Meguro Station in Tokyo. The Meguro Station also has a private railroad station side by side, and the train passes only about 10 meters from the rear wall of the church. Before renovation, as the train passed by, the noise level in the church reached 55 to 60 dB(A). The sound system was also not effective due to the long reverberation time in the sanctuary.

After acoustical investigation, the following plans for improvement were presented:
    1) increase of the sound insulation of the windows,
    2) sound absorbing treatment of ceiling and walls,
    3) replacement of the loudspeaker system.

The sound insulation of the windows was improved by adding a glass pane 6 mm thick on the inner side of the existing windows. The noise level in the church was then decreased by about 5 to 10 dB(A).

The sound absorbing treatment was installed on part of the ceiling and the walls using glass wool sheets. The reverberation time was reduced from approximately 6 seconds to 4 seconds at 500 Hz.

Six loudspeaker and time-delay units were installed to get sufficient direct-to-reverberant energy ratio. As a result, the acoustic gain has been increased and speech intelligibility has been greatly improved, even in the empty condition.

St. ANSELM's PRIORY
TOKYO JAPAN
RENOVATED – 1983

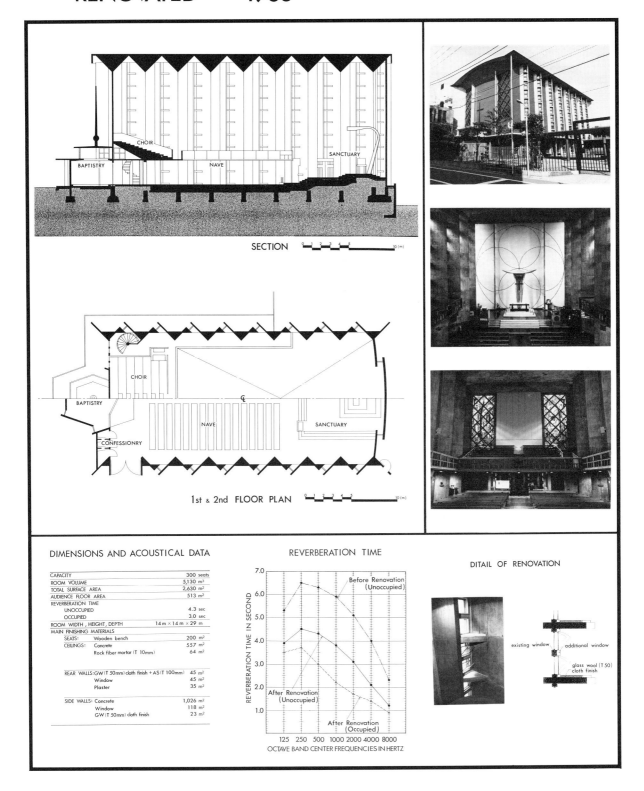

SECTION   0 1 2 3 4 5   10 (m)

1st & 2nd FLOOR PLAN   0 1 2 3 4 5   10 (m)

BAPTISTRY CHOIR NAVE SANCTUARY

CONFESSIONRY

DIMENSIONS AND ACOUSTICAL DATA

CAPACITY		300 seats
ROOM VOLUME		5,130 m³
TOTAL SURFACE AREA		2,630 m²
AUDIENCE FLOOR AREA		513 m²
REVERBERATION TIME		
	UNOCCUPIED	4.3 sec
	OCCUPIED	3.0 sec
ROOM WIDTH , HEIGHT, DEPTH		14 m × 14 m × 29 m
MAIN FINISHING MATERIALS		
SEATS:	Wooden bench	200 m²
CEILINGS:	Concrete	557 m²
	Rock fiber mortar (T 10mm)	64 m²
REAR WALLS:	GW (T 50mm) cloth finish + AS (T 100mm)	45 m²
	Window	45 m²
	Plaster	35 m²
SIDE WALLS:	Concrete	1,026 m²
	Window	118 m²
	GW (T 50mm) cloth finish	23 m²

REVERBERATION TIME

Before Renovation (Unoccupied)

After Renovation (Unoccupied)

After Renovation (Occupied)

REVERBERATION TIME IN SECOND

125 250 500 1000 2000 4000 8000
OCTAVE BAND CENTER FREQUENCIES IN HERTZ

DITAIL OF RENOVATION

existing window   additional window

glass wool (T 50) cloth finish

ST. IGNATIUS CHURCH
TOKYO, JAPAN

RENOVATION COMPLETED: 1982

OWNER: Catholic Church Japan

ARCHITECT: Gropper

ACOUSTICAL CONSULTANT: Minoru Nagata & Associates
                               Tokyo, Japan

St. Ignatius Church is a famous Catholic church in Yotsuya, one of the heaviest traffic
locations in Tokyo. Church members had complained for a long time about the difficulty
of understanding speech. At the request of the Church, an acoustical investigation was
carried out in 1972 by M. Nagata Acoustic Engineer and Associates.

From this investigation, two main factors which cause the deterioration of speech intelligibility were found. They are:

    1) excessive reverberation in the concave sanctuary
    2) the increase of reverberant sound energy by distributed loudspeakers on the wall.

    Sound absorbing treatment was installed on the wall of the sanctuary in 1974. The
sound absorbing structures were designed to be effective only for the middle frequency
range. The reverberation time was then reduced from 3.5 seconds to 2.8 seconds at 500
Hz.

Improvement of the performance of the sound system was carried out in 1982. The two
central systems were installed as a main loudspeaker system and their frequency characteristics were adjusted by subjective tests.

With these improvements, stability against acoustic feedback was increased and also
speech intelligibility was greatly improved.

St. IGNATIUS CHURCH
TOKYO JAPAN
RENOVATED — 1982

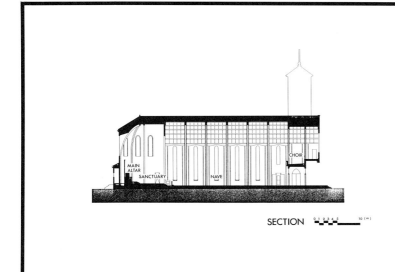

SECTION

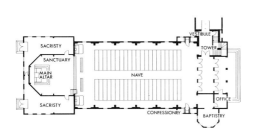

1st FLOOR PLAN

DIMENSIONS AND ACOUSTICAL DATA

CAPACITY		420 seats
ROOM VOLUME		5,100 m³
TOTAL SURFACE AREA		2,130 m²
AUDIENCE FLOOR AREA		380 m²
REVERBERATION TIME		
UNOCCUPIED		2.8 sec
OCCUPIED		2.0 sec
ROOM WIDTH , HEIGHT, DEPTH		14 m × 14 m × 43 m
MAIN FINISHING MATERIALS		
SEATS:	Wooden bench	187 m²
CEILINGS:	Plaster	504 m²
REAR WALLS:	Plaster	108 m²
	Door	12 m²
	Window	13 m²
	Opening	16 m²
SIDE WALLS:	Plaster	414 m²
	Window	72 m²

REVERBERATION TIME

Before Renovation (Unoccupied)

After Renovation (Unoccupied)

After Renovation (Occupied)

REVERBERATION TIME IN SECOND

125 250 500 1000 2000 4000 8000
OCTAVE BAND CENTER FREQUENCIES IN HERTZ

SANCTUARY (AFTER RENOVATION)

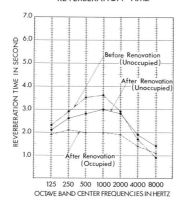

← sprayed rock wool

INDEX OF ACOUSTICAL CONSULTANTS

PHOTOGRAPHIC CREDITS

Page

4	William Herrin
6	Courtesy: Laser, Knight, Hathaway and Guest
8	D. A. Paoletti
10	Rob Super
12	A. K. Yeap
14, 16	Julius Schulman
18	Wayne Thom; E. A. Wetherill
20	Wayne Thom
22	Robert Brandeis
24	Tim Street-Porter
26	Carl Gaede
28	Michael Denny
30	---
32	E. A. Wetherill; Stanford University Archive; Peter Henricks
34, 36	B. Y. Kinzey, Jr.
38	---
40	M. Long
42, 74	D. Joiner
44, 46, 48	Daniel P. Prusinowski
50	Duke University Archive; Thad Sparks
52	Courtesy: Jaffe Acoustics Inc.
54	Daniel W. Martin
56, 58	A. Campanella
60, 62, 64, 66	E. A. Daly
68	Stan Franzos
70	Courtesy: Newcomb & Boyd
72	Lou Rheems
76	Michael K. Sullivan
78	R. Richards
80	Vern H. Delgatty
82	Oscar Tijerina Garga
84	Katzuji Naniwa and Minoru Nagata
86	Hideo Nakamura
88	Katzuji Naniwa